KT-419-409

Jesus the Christ

BY THE SAME AUTHOR:

Articles of the Church of England
Historicity of the Gospels
Jesus, Master and Lord
The Meaning of the Cross
The Patristic Doctrine of Redemption
The Pattern of Christian Truth
Thomas and Evangelists (with Hugh Montefiore)

MOWBRAYS THEOLOGICAL LIBRARY

Jesus the Christ

H. E. W. Turner

Sometime Fellow of Lincoln College, Oxford; Canon of Durham; and van Mildert Professor of Divinity in the University of Durham

MOWBRAYS LONDON & OXFORD

© H. E. W. Turner 1976

First Published 1976
by A. R. Mowbray & Co. Ltd.
The Alden Press, Osney Mead
Oxford OX2 0EG

ISBN 0 264 66255 5

Printed in Great Britain
at the Alden Press, Oxford

Acknowledgements

My thanks are due to the following, for permission to quote in this volume from works of which they control the copyright: Cambridge University Press (John Knox, 'The Humanity and Divinity of Christ', A. R. Vidler (ed.), Soundings); Faber & Faber Limited (D. M. Baillie, *God Was in Christ*); Longman Group Limited (E. L. Mascall, *Christ, the Christian and the Church*); Macmillan, London and Basingstoke (William Temple, *Christus Veritas*); Nisbet & Company Limited (W. N. Pittenger, *The Word Incarnate*); SCM Press Limited (J. A. T. Robinson, *The Human Face of God*); SPCK (G. L. Prestige, *Fathers and Heretics*).

H. E. W. Turner

Eskdale, April 1975.

Introduction to Mowbrays Library of Theology

The last quarter of the twentieth century is a good time for the Christian Church to take stock of its beliefs. In the course of the century, Christian theology has had many challenges to meet—and has itself not remained unchanged by the encounter. Society has become more pluralist and less committed; dogmatism is at a discount. Christianity has had to survive in a climate which regards its beliefs as matters of opinion rather than of fact, and in a world not readily convinced of their relevance either to public politics or private morals. Within the faith (and particularly in the sixties of the century) there have been radical questionings of almost every aspect of doctrine.

Despite all this, there are signs that people are more willing now than they were a decade or so ago to listen to more constructive voices. Christians need to state how they can—as men of their own age and culture, and as heirs to the radical ferment of ideas which characterised the mid-century—articulate a faith in God, Father, Son and Holy Spirit, hold convictions about the nature of man and his destiny, and show the relevance of belief to conduct. The contributors to this series think it their duty to give as plain and straightforward a statement as is compatible with their intellectual integrity of what the Christian faith is, and how it can be honestly and meaningfully expressed today.

Christian faith has always been the faith of a community. It is therefore necessary to 'earth' such an articulation in terms of a particular community of Christians. So the contributors to this series are all Anglicans, confident that theirs is a particular expression of the universal faith which still merits serious consideration. The series therefore aims to reflect, not only themes of interest to all Christians at all times, but also particular aspects of Christian theology which are currently exercising the Church of England in congregations and Synods. And, since there will always be rival religions and ideologies competing for men's allegiance, we need to explore their claims and ask what the attitude of Anglicans is towards them. But that the Church has a faith which is worth stating and that it is a faith to live by, is a convinction shared by every contributor.

Michael Perry

Contents

1 Introducing Christology

'CHRISTIANITY is Christ.' We have often been told this, and many of us have found it true in our own experience. Herbert Butterfield, formerly Regius Professor of Modern History at Cambridge, once expressed this truth with great simplicity and directness in the words, 'Hold to Christ, and for the rest be totally uncommitted.'

The centrality of Christ was characteristic of the faith and practice of the early Church. The creed-like slogan 'Jesus Christ is Lord' (1 Cor. 12.3; cf. 8.6) marked off the new People of God from Jew and pagan alike. The cryptogram of the fish, which in Greek represents the initial letters of the phrase 'Jesus Christ, Son of God, Saviour', was the distinguishing 'recognition signal' between Christians. Even pagan writers were aware of the special valuation assigned to Christ by Christians. About AD 120 the younger Pliny, governor of a Roman province, who had no previous knowledge of the sect, writing a letter of inquiry to the Roman Emperor and asking how its members should be treated, tells us that Christians 'sing hymns to Christ as to God' (or 'a god'). During the excavation of the Palatine Palace at Rome, there was discovered on the walls of the pages' Common Room a rough drawing of a man kneeling before a figure on a cross, bearing an ass's head. The scrawled legend was, 'Alexamenus worships his god'. That Jesus was Lord and therefore to be worshipped is the 'given', more fundamental than any doctrine, from which Christology starts, but in the long run it required a doctrine to explain and support it. This is the starting-point of Christology, not the goal which the theologian hopes to reach.

The fact of Christ as Lord is the focal point of Christianity and its distinguishing feature among world religions.

1

Christology is the term applied to the doctrine of the Person and work of Christ. If the Christian claim for Christ is to be upheld, who or what is he? The terms in which it is expressed, the lengths to which the inquiry has been carried, will sometimes appear remote when they are compared with its simple and direct starting-point. The reader may find his attention flagging in the effort to follow the different ways in which the doctrine has been stated and the controversies in which Christians have been engaged over the centuries. If he thinks of these as attempts to 'capture a spring' or to explore a mystery, he will have patience to proceed. Those who framed the various christologies which we shall study together all believed that they were saying something true and important about Christ and attempting to explore his meaning and significance.

It is not surprising that more than one point of entry into Christology has been found. Many have found that the best way of exploring 'the manifold riches of Christ' is to start from the side of God. All would agree that the initiative in counsel and will belongs to God and would exclude the notion that the fact of Christ can be explained merely as a realisation by man of his own powers and possibilities by his own unaided efforts. Most theologians in the past have considered that this implies a divine descent into human existence, though some recent thinkers consider that the divine initiative is sufficiently safeguarded if Jesus can be described as the man of God's own choosing. All accept again that God is involved in Jesus as the Christ but considerable differences exist in the manner and extent of this divine involvement. For one great tradition this must imply that the central core of the incarnate Lord was 'in essence all divine', for others it is sufficient to claim that God was related to Jesus in a unique degree. 'The Word was made flesh', 'God was in Christ'. Even in the New Testament different emphases seem to be set before us.

But some have claimed that a christology from the side of man can offer a satisfactory account of the Incarnation. The disciples first approached him as a man and only gradually came to realise after the Resurrection that more than this was involved. His human experiences recorded in the gospels, his

sufferings, trouble of soul, agony and temptations must be fully
real if the fact of Christ is to have relevance and significance
for us. They have a direct bearing not only on the doctrine of
his Person, who or what Jesus was, but also on his Work, the
Redemption and New Life which he brought to men. A
starting-point from the side of man could not therefore be
automatically exluded.

There are then two solidarities in Jesus the Christ: his
solidarity with God and with ourselves. He is solid with God,
for he came forth from the side of God and God was involved
with him. He revealed God and gave to his disciples the answer
to vital questions like 'What is God like?' 'What is he doing?'
and 'How is his Kingdom to be understood and entered?'. But
there is also a solidarity with man. He showed what man was
intended by God to be and how he is meant to live. The theme
of the Imitation of Christ has been a constant inspiration for
Christian living. His experience as man not only rose to the
full heights of human possibilities but also plumbed the depths
of man's inhumanity to man. In Christology these two
solidarities must be asserted together, but the relation between
them and the choice to be made if they appear to conflict with
each other have been matters of high debate. Later Christology
spoke of Jesus the Christ as 'True God and True Man' (or, in
the older translation with which many will be more familiar,
'Very God and Very Man'). Christology will need to ask
questions about the content and implications of this statement.

Oversimplifications naturally arose; and these upset the
balance of the doctrine and made it more difficult, instead of
easier, to explain the Christian estimate of Christ. Docetism
claimed that Jesus was not really man but only God play-
acting as a man. This might satisfy his solidarity with God but
left his solidarity with us completely in the air. It made nonsense of his recorded human experiences. For many centuries
in the exegesis of the gospels there were traces of what has been
called a psychological docetism; a flinching away from the full
content and value of his human experiences and an attempt to
make them less shocking to his divinity. Thus Cyril of
Alexandria interprets the human progress of Christ as a
gradual self-disclosure of God the Logos and coins the

ingenious paradox, 'He suffered impassibly' to describe his
passional experiences. *Adoptionism* spoke of Jesus as a mere
man who at some point, whether at his Baptism or his
Resurrection, became what he was not before and was given a
new divine or quasi-divine status. This raised difficulties for the
doctrine of God as well as gravely understating the divine
involvement in Christ. Others tended to express their doctrine
of Christ in terms of a hybrid figure, part God and part man, a
mediator between God and man and therefore not fully either
but something of both. Without necessarily going to such
lengths some christologians used analogies drawn from
physical mixtures, whether liquid or solid, to express the close
unity between the two solidarities in Christ. Such a 'heraldic
Christ', like the wyverns or griffins of heraldry, cannot satisfy
the needs of Christology. Christ is the mediator between God
and man, not by being a bit of both but by being both at once.
Nor is he a kind of schizophrene, God and man alternately
without any closer relationship between the two solidarities.
While this was never put forward as a formal Christology,
certainly not in psychological jargon, there are statements even
by orthodox theologians which seem to imply a Box and Cox
alternation between the two natures. The christologian often
feels himself to be walking a veritable tightrope, seeking to
avoid these and other pitfalls and yet trying to steer a straight
course. It is not surprising that the root problem in Christology
is how to provide a satisfactory account of the unity of the
Person of Christ and yet to satisfy the conditions of the two
solidarities.

   Like all other doctrines Christology requires an intellectual
framework within which to expound it. This must be drawn
from the best secular thought of the day. But here a further
difficulty arises since no framework has been devised solely or
primarily for the purposes of the theologian. Here three
patterns of thought will concern us. The thought of the Bible
itself is not primarily philosophical. It employs images rich in
background and meaning rather than concepts clear and
precise in content. They are evocative rather than descriptive
in character. In the closing years of the Old Testament period
and in New Testament times the biblical images were subjected

to the influences of Greek philosophy and began to acquire a more stable and definable significance. At first tentatively, but later with increasing confidence, the theologians of the Church took over the framework of secular philosophy. Care was however needed lest in the process of restatement something of vital importance might be subtracted from the doctrines themselves. The object of the exercise was to provide a more stable framework for the biblical realities. Its main thrust was ontological (ontology is the description of being by means of metaphysical and logical concepts), and it led to the use in Christology of words such as those translated into English as 'substance', 'nature', and 'person', though, as we shall see, the exact shade of meaning has to be carefully understood, and any translation is bound to be to some extent misleading. Recently the validity of this whole approach has been questioned by theologians and the search for a more dynamic approach in terms of relationships has become fashionable. Modern psychology rather than classical ontology has become the indispensable instrument of Christology. Care must therefore be taken to distinguish between the classical use of 'Person' which denotes the logical or metaphysical centre of a subject and the modern usage of 'personality' which casts its net more widely and includes relationships and, in the opinion of some psychologists, is even constructed from them. Terms like substance and nature are, rightly or wrongly, suspected by the new approach as unduly static in character and are replaced by words like activity, operation and function. Though these were by no means neglected by the classical framework, they were assigned a dependent and sometimes even a subordinate role. We shall need to test for adequacy, or to consider whether the new framework can provide for all that needs to be said under the head of Christology.

We shall not be able to confine our attention to strictly christological questions. That is because, while Christology is the focal point of Christian theology, it is closely related to all other doctrines. Coherence is no negligible criterion of Christian as well as other truth. We shall therefore need to watch the effects upon Christology of changes of emphasis in the doctrine of God. Since the Person and Work of Christ are closely related to each other, we shall need to keep our eyes open for the requirements of the doctrine of Redemption. No doctrine of the Person of Christ can be acceptable unless it supports or sheds light on the experience of being redeemed by Christ. This is the meaning of a phrase which will be often used in this book: the 'redemptive control' on Christology. The theologian will test his christology by its repercussions on the doctrine of Redemption, much as a scientist will use an experiment performed under test conditions to verify his conclusions. Significantly, though less directly, there is a similarity of pattern between Christology and the doctrine of Grace, the nature and scope of the redemptive activity of God in human lives and the life of the Church. These related doctrines will be the subject of a separate chapter, but they will concern us at various points in our discussion of Christology proper.

This book is an attempt to guide the reader through some at least of the main contributions to Christology. It is therefore to some extent a historical study, picking out key figures and movements from New Testament times onwards. Inevitably much has had to be omitted, but the primary aim has been to set out the issues which affect our choice of the best and most adequate discussions of the doctrine and to help the reader towards a clearer insight into the meaning and significance of Jesus the Christ and thereby (God willing) to a deeper and more discerning discipleship of our Lord.

2 The witness of the New Testament to Christ

THE unity of the New Testament is to be found in its witness to Christ, the fact and meaning of Jesus as the Christ. Yet this unity of witness is compatible with a variety of insights into his Person and Work. This diversity was inevitable, for the fact of Jesus—living, dying and risen—was the great new event on which the Church was founded, and the New Testament writers were seeking images and thought-forms adequate to express his significance. As every aspect of religion and life was related to Christ and revalued in the process, we can expect to find a growing sense of his meaning as the fact of Christ was applied to an ever-widening context.

We must begin with the Old Testament. Jesus himself was nurtured in the Old Testament and the first disciples naturally looked here for their earliest sources for the understanding of Jesus. In the long run however the Church was led beyond the Old Testament, not only because its original Jewish constituency was replaced by an increasingly Gentile membership, but also because the Old Testament thought-forms by themselves could not provide an adequate framework for the significance of the Christ who had come.

The Old Testament is a book of promise and fulfilment grouped mainly round a series of titles such as Messiah (Christ in Greek), Son of Man and the Servant of the Lord. Yet even these formed a kind of 'moving target' since, during the last two centuries BC, considerable development took place which continued within the first Christian century. The term 'Messiah', used of the human agent in the fulfilment of the divine promise, was increasingly understood in a political sense as the Jews became subservient to foreign rulers. The title 'Son of Man', already used somewhat broadly by Ezekiel

7

and in the Psalms, describes the faithful remnant under persecution in Daniel and becomes the heavenly champion of Israel in 1 Enoch. Even within a single document (Isa. 40–55) the concept of 'the Servant of the Lord' changes from Israel as a whole through the faithful nucleus of the People of God to expectations which could only be fulfilled in a single and unique individual. The theme of promise and fulfilment could not therefore be applied in a mechanical way by drawing up a list of 'fulfilment specifications' and matching them with the figure of Jesus. God's provision and man's expectations worked on different principles. The one who came was not less but greater than man looked for. Yet the Church was not in error in looking within the Old Testament for clues towards the understanding of Jesus, even if in the long run it found itself bound to transcend Jewish thought-forms and to look elsewhere for its principal tools.

God's promise was fulfilled in Christ. It would therefore seem natural to begin with the gospels and to use them as a kind of historical 'control' over the rest of the New Testament. But this is only partly possible and cannot by itself prove decisive. For the gospels are not insulated from the rest of the New Testament witness to Christ. They were written by believers for believers, and therefore form part of that witness. Certainly they contain most of the historical data for the life of Jesus but in the forms of witness, not of a historical source-book. The older 'Quest of the Historical Jesus', which came to an abrupt and final end with Schweitzer's devastating book (1910), rested on the false premise of a historical nucleus which could be disentangled from the witness of the Church. The falsity of this premise does not necessarily destroy the historical value of the gospels but their purpose conditions the form in which this history is presented. Their subject is Jesus and not primarily the Church, and each evangelist in his own way testified that it was Jesus who was the Christ.

A new quest for the historical Jesus, freed from the dubious assumptions of the previous inquiry, offers more modest, yet more promising, results. The first point can be made in the form of a quotation from the Anglo-American philosopher A. N. Whitehead (1861–1947) in his book *Religion in the Making*

(p. 56). Comparing the lives of the Buddha and the Christ as two illuminating moments in the history of mankind, he wrote: 'The Buddha gave his doctrine to enlighten the world; Christ gave his life. It is for Christians to discern the doctrine'. Jesus himself was not primarily a christologian. His main teaching concerned not his own Person but the Kingdom of God. We cannot however doubt that he had a self-awareness not only of his message but of his right to give it and his own relation to it. Only at rare moments can we trace in the gospels evidence for his self-consciousness or development within it. The Baptism marks his setting apart for his Messianic vocation and the Voice from Heaven 'This is my beloved Son in whom I am well pleased' (Mark. 1.11), drawn partly from the Psalms and partly from the Servant passages in Isa. 40–55, gives the seal of divine approval on the dedication of his beloved or unique Son. The Transfiguration similarly seals a new stage in his ministry. After the Confession of Peter that Jesus is the Christ it opens the way for a new stage in Christ's teaching that Messiahship must be understood in terms of suffering and not of earthly triumph. Moses and Elijah appear as two 'supporters', representing the Law and the Prophets, and the glory is not only a sign of divine approval but also a foretaste of the Resurrection which lies on the other side of the Passion. The incident begins the build-up for the Passion which, especially in Mark, is the true climax of the gospel. It has often been pointed out that Mark takes the form of an extended Passion narrative with a long introduction setting the figure of the Crucified in context and in focus. Evidence for the inner life of Jesus, and particularly his inner conflict, is almost entirely confined to the Temptation Narratives of Matthew and Luke and the Passion narratives of all three synoptists. It is a mark of the reserve of the gospels that this should be the case.

The titles used by Jesus are however sufficient evidence that he knew what was about and that his role as an authoritative teacher, charismatic miracle-worker and seeker of souls was firmly rooted in the Old Testament. While some scholars are doubtful whether these titles are authentic to Jesus, I have given reasons elsewhere for regarding them as an authentic part of the Gospel tradition (H. E. W. Turner, *Jesus Master and*

Lord, pp. 185–235. A. R. Mowbray, 1953). The title Messiah
or Christ is used rather on the lips of others as a conjecture
about his role or an affirmation about him than by Jesus
himself. In no recorded case however does Jesus disclaim
Messiahship. He accepts Peter's Confession but directs his
further teaching to the new content which he gives to the title.
In Mark 14.62 he answers the High Priest's adjuration 'Art
thou the Christ, the Son of the Blessed?' with a strong
affirmative, but adds a further qualification drawn from the
concept of the Son of Man. Jesus is all the Messiah there is, all
the Messiah there is going to be, but he looks elsewhere for his
most distinctive title. This may be due to a Messianic cross-
purpose between Jesus and his contemporaries, many of whom
looked for a national liberator. Others have written of a veiled
Messiahship or of a Messianic Secret to resolve the difficulty.
His favourite self-designation, the 'Son of Man', is certainly
authentic in view of its infrequent use, even by way of allusion,
in the rest of the New Testament. It occurs in two widely
different contexts of suffering and glory. These are closely
related to the themes of Humiliation and Exaltation which
recur elsewhere in the New Testament, though not associated
with the title. Whether the concept of the Suffering Servant had
an independent influence on the mind of Jesus is a question
hotly debated by scholars. At least the note of suffering is
included under the title 'Son of Man'. More important are the
linked concepts of the Father and the Son. While this is
distinctive of the Fourth Gospel, there are some significant
dovetails in the synoptic tradition, in a passage in Mark
(13.32; cf. Matt. 24.36) on the ignorance of the date of the
Second Coming and in an important saying of the Johannine
type in the non-Marcan source common to Matthew and Luke
(Matt. 11.27; Luke 10.22): 'No man knoweth the Son save the
Father, nor the Father save the Son, and him to whom the Son
willeth to reveal him.' We have already noted that the Voice
from Heaven both at the Baptism and the Transfiguration adds
the important qualifier 'beloved' (which has the additional
nuance of 'unique') to the word 'Son'. The word '*Abba*',
reminiscent of the prayer usage of Jesus himself, left
untranslated in Mark 14.36 and recalled by Paul (Gal. 4.6;

Rom. 8.15), is an unusual form expressing a unique intimacy with God. This agrees with other uses of the word 'Father' used of God by Jesus in the gospels. He is 'My Father', 'Your Father', 'the Father', never 'Our Father' in a sense which includes both Jesus and his disciples. The Matthean version of the Lord's Prayer is introduced by the words 'And when *ye* pray, say "Our Father".' It is clear then that, while the titles of Jesus start within the Old Testament, they are revalued by his application of them to himself.

The third notable feature of the historical Jesus which comes clearly through the gospel witness is a distinctive life-style. His humanity is clear enough. That is where the disciples started in their understanding of him. Terms like teacher (*rabbi*), prophet and, at the furthest, Messiah, mark their understanding of him. Their starting-point was the human, though the exceptional and charismatic human. For the most part they remained loyal, though baffled; obedient, yet amazed. But in Jesus himself there is also a first-hand note of authority which contrasted sharply with the derivative character of much contemporary Jewish teaching. Jesus not only set aside much of the Oral Tradition of the Law, especially the Sabbath regulations, but even, according to Matthew, deepened some aspects of the Mosaic Law itself. 'Ye have heard that it was said by them of old time . . . but I say unto you' (Matt. 5.21, 27, 31, 33, 38, 43). The self-designation 'I am', typical of the Fourth Gospel, again has dovetails in the synoptic tradition. At the stilling of the storm (Mark 6.50) the words of Jesus are better rendered 'Fear not I AM' as an expression of his mastery over the forces of nature. In his reply to the High Priest quoted above Jesus answers 'I AM' followed by a prediction of the glory of the Son of Man at his coming. The context suggests something more than a mere 'Yes'. The third passage refers not to Jesus himself but to false Messiahs who make a similar protestation. Nothing is more characteristic of Jesus than the formula 'Amen, Amen I say unto you'. For a devout Jew 'Amen' was a response of acceptance or obedience to the divine will. Its use by Jesus to preface parts of his teaching seems to indicate that he stood on the other side of divine ordinance and human response. Paul seems to recall this usage

in his description of Jesus as God's 'Amen' to his promises (2
Cor. 1.20). The freshness and authority of his teaching on the
Kingdom of God invites the comment of some Greek fathers
that Jesus is the Kingdom or the King himself. Jesus is not
brought or 'thrown up' by the Kingdom. Rather he brings the
Kingdom with himself. His profound intuitive knowledge of
men, enemies as well as friends, seems to go beyond the limits
of what might be called 'holy shrewdness'. Here, as at other
points, the Fourth Gospel makes explicit what I have called
elsewhere the 'hinterland of divinity' behind a foreground of
humanity. The 'veiled Messiah', the Suffering Son of Man is at
the same time the revealer of the Father which makes him our
most reliable clue to the character of God. But this at once
opens the way for Christology. If God is Christlike, who then
is Jesus? That is a question which the gospels force upon us
and to which their witness in various ways seeks to provide an
answer. If Jesus was not himself a christologian, his recorded
teaching and ministry support and necessitate further
christological explorations on the part of the Church.

The watershed for the understanding of Jesus was the
Resurrection. It is a mark of the scrupulous reserve of the
evangelists that they never attempt to describe the event itself.
In the gospels it is made known by its effects and attendant
circumstances—the Empty Tomb (a primitive and widespread
tradition); the Post-Resurrection Appearances, without which
the Empty Tomb would not be a gospel, but an enigma; and
above all, the continuing impact of 'this same Jesus' (Acts
1.11) on his disciples and the wider circles of the Christian
Church. It has been well pointed out that it is not simply a
Resurrection, but the Resurrection of this superbly good man
which was decisive. The differences, and even the
discrepancies, within the gospel narratives arise partly from
the interpretations of the evangelists themselves but mainly
because the Resurrection itself is the event too big for history
which through the act of God has got into history. The post-
incarnate impact of Jesus made the task of Christology more
urgent by adding a new dimension which needed to be explored
and taken into account. No longer was it simply a matter of
the earthly life and teaching of Jesus but also his continuing

presence and power, self-identical but in a different idiom, which became its subject-matter.

Three points of special significance for New Testament Christology emerged almost immediately after the Resurrection and must be taken closely in connection with the event itself. The Resurrection was seen as the vindication of Jesus; the assurance that his Cross and Passion were not his final defeat but the prelude to his victory. It was, as it were, in act what the Voice from Heaven at the Baptism and the Transfiguration were in word—God's 'This is my beloved Son in whom I am well pleased.' This was expressed in the form of imagery as the Exaltation of Jesus to the right hand of God. We need not stumble at the idea of ascent as if God were literally aloft in the sky or that he actually possessed a right hand. Its intention is evocative rather than descriptive, and expresses the return of Jesus to the glory of the Father after his earthly work was complete. The lowliness and suffering of Jesus and his victory ratified by God through the Resurrection were now combined into a single pattern of Humiliation and Exaltation. Clear evidence for this first step towards a Christology, natural enough for a group of believers moving from earthly discipleship into a new experience of the Risen Christ, is to be found in the early sermons in Acts. If we cannot completely exclude the view that they may be free compositions of the author of Acts after the manner of secular historians, they seem none the less to contain genuine primitive elements and do not reflect the Christology of the author himself. C. H. Dodd, sometime Professor of Divinity at Cambridge and the leading authority of his day on the gospels, found no difficulty in using their content for his reconstruction of the primitive Kerugma or Gospel Proclamation. In the Sermon of Peter in Acts 2 Jesus is described as 'a man approved by God unto you by mighty works ... delivered up (to death) by the determinate counsel and foreknowledge of God (verses 22–23) and the effect of the Resurrection was that 'God has made this Jesus whom you crucified both Lord and Christ' (verse 36). Jesus then is the predestinate man, 'the man of God's own choosing' and the Resurrection leads to an Exaltation Christology which sees in him a man exalted to a

more than human status or form of being. Other passages
which may imply the same idea are Romans 1.4, 'Declared' or
'Made' (the participle is variously translated) 'the Son of God
according to the spirit of holiness by the Resurrection from the
dead'; and (on one interpretation) Phil. 2.5–11 where the
climax of Exaltation is linked with the conferment of 'the name
above every name', the title Lord. If the Resurrection is not
explicitly mentioned in this passage it is certainly not excluded.
There is then some evidence in the New Testament for the
existence of an Exaltation Christology. It would however be
too strong to describe this as Adoptionism or the view that
Jesus was 'adopted' as the Son of God at some point in history
(either the Baptism or the Resurrection) to become what he
was not before: a more than human being. It does not represent
a formal christology, but only the first steps towards a
christology which would need to be reinforced by other strands
before it could be adequately clarified.

The second development was the application of the title
'Lord' to Jesus. That it antedates the Greek environment of the
Church seems to be proved by the eschatological or liturgical
acclamation '*Maranatha*' ('Come Lord' or 'Our Lord comes')
preserved in its Aramaic form (1 Cor. 16.22; cf. Rev. 22.20 in
Greek). It implies not only obedience but also worship and
adoration. In Hellenistic circles it was applied in cultic
contexts to gods or men to whom an attitude of worship was
appropriate. It was used for example of gods who formed the
centre of a Mystery Cult, such as Demeter at Eleusis, or in the
widespread cult of the Egyptian deities Isis, Osiris and Serapis.
It was also applied to a Roman Emperor who was revered as a
god in the eastern half of the Mediterranean world. Paul
contrasts the 'gods many and lords many' of paganism with
the 'one God and Lord Jesus Christ' of the early Church (1
Cor. 8.5–6). The confession of Christ as Lord was alike the
battle-cry and the rallying-point of the primitive Christians. Of
even greater importance was the use of the term 'Lord' for the
divine name Jahweh in the Septuagint or the Greek translation
of the Old Testament. In Phil. 2 the content of the 'name above
every name' is spelt out in language drawn from Isa. 45.23 in
the Septuagint. That the title 'Lord' as applied to Jesus belongs

to the Post-Resurrection period is confirmed by the evidence of the gospels themselves. Mark, true to his aim of aligning us with the first disciples whose blindness and disobedience is a constant theme, uses the title sparingly. Apart from the vocative as a respectful address to Jesus, without further overtones, it only occurs in three passages (Mark 5.19; 11.3 and 12.35–7). In Mark 5.19 the Gadarene demoniac is bidden to declare what great things the Lord has done for him. In view of the mixed racial and religious character of the district this is better interpreted as a reference to Jahweh than to Jesus. In Mark 11.3 the disciples are bidden to tell the owner of the colt 'the Lord has need of him' where a possible paraphrase is some such phrase as 'on the King's business' or the familiar OHMS. The context of Mark 12.35–7 lies within an exegesis of Ps. 110. The only significant Matthean reference relates to the Risen Christ (Matt. 28.6). Luke on the other hand uses the title fourteen times where a direct feedback from Post-Resurrection usage is probable.

The third development which has recently become a matter of debate between scholars is the concept of pre-existence. This has normally been taken to imply that before his earthly life Jesus, or rather his divine nature, pre-existed as God the Son from eternity with the Father. This has become a built-in feature of the classical doctrine of the Incarnation. We are only concerned here with its origin and development in New Testament times. The American scholar John Knox admits that the concepts arose at least within a few decades of the Resurrection as a simple theological reflex of the Post-incarnate impact of the Risen Lord. The author to the Hebrews writes of 'Jesus Christ, the same yesterday, to-day and for ever' (Heb. 13.8). In the light of the Resurrection it became unthinkable that, in whatever sense, there could ever have been a time when Jesus had not existed. Initially no doubt the precise definition of who or what pre-existed was not directly raised, and further explorations both within the New Testament and later would be necessary before its full implications could be grasped. It occurs at first in quite untheological contexts which do not give the impression that a new and highly controversial point is being made. Thus Paul

can write 'Though he was rich, yet he became poor' (2 Cor.
8.9) and 'God sending his own Son in the likeness of sinful
flesh and for sin' (Rom. 8.3).

The problem is, what does this pre-existence mean and how
can it be related convincingly to the genuine humanity of
Jesus? Some older scholars called attention to the use of the
concepts of pre-existence to describe whatever was of ultimate
religious concern. Thus in late Judaism angels were regarded
as circumcised and kept the Sabbath. They were believed to
have given the Law to Moses, a tradition used by Paul to
discredit rather than to enhance its authority (Gal. 3.19).
Possibly an earlier move in this direction may be found in Ps.
119.89: 'O Lord, thy word [the Law] abideth for ever in
heaven'. But it is a long way from this special designation of
institutions to affirmations about a Person.

Both John Knox and Bishop J. A. T. Robinson regard the
idea of pre-existence as one way of expressing the significance
of Jesus as the predestinate man; the man of God's
foreknowledge. They argue that in the long run 'We can have
the humanity without the pre-existence, and we can have the
pre-existence without the humanity. There is absolutely no way
of having both' (John Knox, *The Humanity and the Divinity of
Christ*, Cambridge, 1967, p. 106). This is a sweeping and far-
reaching judgement which it is difficult to reconcile with the
evidence of the New Testament itself. The material used to
explore the meaning of pre-existence, and the uses to which the
concept was put, fail to substantiate this statement.

In the gospels themselves the concept of pre-existence plays
a relatively small role. The hinterland of divinity is not directly
linked to the idea. Even the Father–Son correlation which
certainly points to a heavenly origin is applied in the gospels
primarily to his present relationship to the Father. This is no
doubt due to their subject-matter; the earthly life and ministry
of our Lord. While Jesus may have known sources which
spoke of the Son of Man as a pre-existent heavenly being, his
use of the title concentrates upon present suffering and future
exaltation and return. In Mark the public ministry opens with
the Baptism and is silent about anything which precedes it. At
one point Luke makes a slight but significant alteration to his

Marcan source. In Mark 1.38 Jesus says of his ministry: 'For this cause I came forth' (presumably from Nazareth). In Luke 4.43 this becomes 'I was sent forth' (presumably from God). The Virgin Birth tradition is inserted by Luke as a kind of appendix at the beginning of his gospel although in Matthew it is more closely integrated into the structure of his gospel. In the Fourth Gospel it is replaced by the Logos Prologue, though the somewhat cumbersome expression of John 1.13 (referring to Christians) 'Which were born, not of blood, nor of the will of the flesh, nor of the will of man, but of God' may be an indirect allusion to the Virgin Birth. The variant reading 'Who was' (singular for plural) is only an attempt to capture the echo. Other New Testament allusions (Gal. 4.4; Heb. 7.3). are scanty and inconclusive. It looks as if pre-existence can be asserted in the New Testament without direct appeal to the Virgin Birth, though the Virgin Birth, which marks off the conception of Jesus as 'the Son of God the most high' (Luke 1.32; 1.35) from the birth of an ordinary human being, strongly suggests pre-existence. On this view the tradition is not a matter of biological curiosity about the human generation of Jesus but a mark of differentiation between the birth of an ordinary mortal and the way in which a pre-existent heavenly being entered the world. Personally I accept the Virgin Birth as a reliable historical tradition and interpret it with Barth as a miracle marking the boundary limit of the Incarnation on the one side, as does the even more significant miracle of the Resurrection on the other. In both, God's seal is set on the Incarnation of his Son in act, as it is in speech at the Baptism and the Transfiguration.

Human foreground and divine hinterland, humanity and pre-existence, a christology from the side of man which starts from the human person of Jesus and interprets the Incarnation as the special indwelling of God in Christ and his vocation (under God) for mankind, and a christology from the side of God which interprets the Incarnation as a divine descent into human life. How were these related and with what different emphases by the main New Testament writers? We must begin with Paul.

The key to Pauline christology is to be found in Rom. 1.3–4

where the one Christ, described as God's Son, can be
approached from two standpoints, 'according to the flesh' and
'according to the spirit of holiness'. This has been called the
earliest christological framework in the New Testament and
contains in germ the distinction between later christologies
from the side of God and from the side of man respectively.
Paul plainly wishes to do justice to both standpoints though
much of his most original thought was devoted to the
exploration of the divine aspect of Christ. Many reasons can
be assigned for this. His conversion followed a vision of the
Risen Christ on the Damascus Road. Chiefly because of their
own intrinsic importance but partly because of the errors
which beset the churches of his foundation, his main
theological preoccupation lay in working out the implications
of the fact of the Resurrection and the concept of pre-existence
which derived from it.

Yet he is in no danger of neglecting the genuine humanity of
Christ. This underlies the important Adam–Christ parallelism
which is repeated with variations in Rom. 5.12–21; 1 Cor.
15.20–2 and possibly Phil. 2.5–11. The context in Rom. 5
concerns Redemption in Christ. Adam is the type of the one
who should come (Christ), Adam the founding father of the old
order, Christ the initiator of the new. From each springs the
appropriate solidarity. The disobedience of Adam leads
through sin to death which entered the world as a result and
henceforth reigns over it. This whole process is reversed in
Christ. The sin, disobedience and transgression of Adam
which ended in death are contrasted with the obedience and
righteousness of Christ with its result, eternal life. The two
solidarities correspond to two kingdoms, of death and of life.
Where sin abounded, grace superabounded. The parallel
depends upon the humanity of Christ and the main emphasis
falls, as we should expect, on Christ rather than on Adam.
While it starts with the redemption of the Christian here and
now, its goals and targets transcend the present. The Pauline
doctrine of salvation through Christ has a strong
eschatological thrust. The argument of the whole chapter is
summarised in its final verse: 'that, as sin reigned in death,
even so might grace reign through righteousness unto eternal

life through Jesus Christ our Lord'.

The same theme recurs in a different context in 1 Cor. 15. The opening verses (21–3) summarise the argument of Rom. 5, but the problem with which Paul is concerned has changed. Instead of the two solidarities, in Adam and in Christ, he discusses the nature of the resurrection body. The contrast between Adam and Christ is brought to bear on the distinction between the earthly and the heavenly; the natural and the spiritual. The superiority of Christ over Adam is again strongly stressed. The first Adam became a living soul, the last Adam (Christ) a life-giving spirit (1 Cor. 15.45). Adam was alive; Christ is lifegiving. Adam was soul (*nephesh* in the Genesis narrative); Christ is spirit (*ruah*; cf. Gen. 1.2). Later the same distinction is pointed slightly differently. 'The first man is of the earth, earthly, the second man is from heaven . . . and, as we have borne the image of the earthly, we shall also bear the image of the heavenly' (1 Cor. 15.47 and 15.49). Here the previous emphasis upon Christ as the Second Adam, who puts into reverse the fatal processes started by the first Adam, is now replaced by the concept of Christ as the Last Adam. The new man in whom is life of Rom. 5 is now described as a lifegiving spirit who confers upon those who are united to him, even while they are on earth, the image of the heavenly. The framework remains the same but the eschatological thrust, which is not absent in Rom. 5 is brought to the fore by the new problem in 1 Cor. 15 of the effects of the Resurrection and the nature of the resurrection body which Christians hope to assume.

In the later Pauline epistles he comes directly to grips with his main christological task: the exploration of the one Christ from the side of God. The theological resources which he uses came from the Old Testament and must be briefly introduced before considering the use which Paul (in common with other New Testament writers) made of them. Under the pressure of a heightened sense of the transcendence of God, the Wisdom Literature of the Old Testament and the Apocrypha picked out for special emphasis certain divine aspects or attributes, the literature is poetic in form and theological rather than philosophical in character, although some books (like the

Wisdom of Solomon) bear traces of Greek influence. Terms
like Wisdom (*hochmah*); Word (*dabar* or *memra*); and, to a
lesser extent, Spirit (*ruah*) are important for our purpose. The
question is whether these attributes or activities are personified
in a graphic semi-poetical manner or whether they are
regarded as personalisations, in some way distinct from God
himself. Do they involve a renumbering within the Godhead or
not? In most cases the Word of God, the Wisdom of God and
the Spirit of God can fairly be paraphrased as 'This is God
speaking, ordering or acting, gripping men and energising
them.' In a few passages however such as Prov. 8 and the
middle chapters of the Book of Wisdom, something more
seems involved. Broadly speaking, the nearer we get to the first
Christian century, the more evident become the traces of
Greek influence in documents emanating from Hellenistic
Judaism (such as the Book of Wisdom and, above all, the
writings of the Alexandrine Jewish philosopher and theologian
Philo), and the closer we get to personalisation. Much depends
again upon the context in which they are employed. The close
link between the Word and the Wisdom and the Law (Torah)
almost necessitates the interpretation of the relevant passages
as personifications, while the application of the Word and the
Wisdom to the pre-incarnate Christ leads inevitably to
something more. The concepts are revalued by their
application to Christ; his significance must not be restricted by
their previous history. We should naturally expect the
application of terms like the Wisdom and the Word to Christ
to lead to a Christology from the side of God rather than that
they should fall conveniently within the limits of a Christology
from the side of man.

The construction of a Christology in Wisdom terms is
largely the contribution of Paul. Christ can be described as 'the
power and the wisdom of God' (1 Cor. 1.24). The 'spiritual
rock', identified with Christ in his exegesis of the wilderness
wanderings of the Exodus, (1 Cor. 10.4) recalls language used
by Philo of the Wisdom.

For a wider application of Wisdom language which lays
bare its Christian motivation we must turn to the Captivity
Epistles. Here Paul uses the Wisdom theme to establish the

relation of Christ to Creation as well as to Redemption. Creation and Redemption (considered as Re-Creation) belong together (cf. Rom. 8.18–23; 2 Cor. 5.17). Hence the concept of the 'cosmic Christ' is central to this group of letters. If Christ is central to Redemption he cannot be excluded from Creation. The claim is made, especially in Colossians and Ephesians (but cf. also Gal. 4.9), that Christ as Lord redeems men not only from Adamic bondage to sin and death, but also from the tyranny of cosmic powers which held many in the Hellenistic world in bondage. In modern terms, Christ saves not only from moral defeat but also from cosmic anxiety. This new step in Christology clearly implies the idea of pre-existence and (despite Robinson) fits a good deal more happily into a Christology from the side of God than into a more man-centred approach. Yet the proclamation of the Lordship of Christ in Creation is still closely related to Redemption through the Cross as the central point of salvation-history.

The key passage here is Col. 1.15–20. It has a hymn-like and poetical character. The first and longer half is concerned with Christ in Creation and owes something to Stoic terminology (verse 17, 'in whom all things consist'; cf. 1 Cor. 8.6). He is 'the image of the invisible God, the firstborn of all creation'. While the term 'image' is applied to Adam in Gen. 1.26, here it seems to be the reciprocal of 'glory', a characteristic later Jewish synonym for God. In Hellenistic Judaism the term 'image' could be applied to the Wisdom. The invisible God is made known through his image, the Wisdom (in this passage, Christ). The next phrase expresses both dignity and temporality. Christ is first, because he is Lord and holds absolute sway over the cosmic powers. He is 'before all things, and in him all things consist'. Pre-existence as well as primacy is included here. This whole section is hard to explain on a predominantly man-centred christology. The second half (verses, 17–20) passes more briefly to Redemption. The unifier of creation of the first half becomes the reconciler between God and man through his death on the Cross and the sphere of reconciliation is the Church. Even when Paul is expounding the theme of the cosmic Christ he is in no danger of forgetting the humanity of Christ.

A further passage in the Captivity Epistles, Phil. 2.5–11, raises greater problems. It is often regarded as a pre-Pauline hymn taken over and used by Paul. Its primary bearing is moral, though in a writer like Paul this does not destroy its christological importance. Two interpretations are possible. Some scholars keep the whole passage within the context of the earthly life of Jesus and find support in the introductory formula 'Let this mind be in you which was also in Christ Jesus' as denoting the subject of the whole passage. In that case it combines the two images of the Second Adam and the Suffering Servant. The 'form of God' recalls the image of God of Gen. 1.26. Unlike Adam, Jesus did not snatch at equality with God (recalling the illusory promise of the Serpent 'Ye shall be as Gods' (Gen. 3.5). The contrasting image of the Servant, more fully expounded, takes over at verse 7 and the climax of the passage is the conferment of the 'name above every name', the title Lord, described in exceedingly high terms and illustrated by the sovereignty of Jesus over all powers in heaven and on earth. On this view then it represents a high statement of Exaltation Christology.

The alternative view, classically expounded by Bishop J. B. Lightfoot in his commentary on Philippians (1868) and supported by many scholars, finds the transition from the pre-existent to the incarnate Christ in verse 7. Pre-existence is implied in verse 6 where a particularly strong participle ('subsisting' rather than 'being') is used in connection with the form of God. This tells against the equation of the 'form of God' with the 'image of God'. Professor Käsemann, a pupil of Bultmann, paraphrases the phrase as, 'having a mode of existence in divine power and substance'. Whether the 'form of God' and 'equality with God' are identified is uncertain. The question depends upon the meaning of the word translated 'robbery' in the Authorised Version. It is unique in the New Testament and is rarely found elsewhere in Greek literature. Two renderings are possible. The first draws a distinction between the form of God and equality with God. The former was already his, but he refused to take the further step of snatching at the latter as a robber grabs his booty. The second identifies the two and runs: 'He did not prize his equality with

God as something to be retained at any cost, as a robber grips his booty tightly for fear of losing it.' The arguments for and against the two views are very evenly balanced. On Lightfoot's interpretation the passage opens with a strong statement of pre-existence; but its main thrust belongs to the incarnate life and falls within salvation-history. This emphasis, together with the moral application of the passage, may serve to explain the description of the ultimate subject as 'Christ Jesus'. The theme of the Imitation of Christ does not contradict his pre-existence as divine but ensures that full weight is given to the Servant who was disclosed as Lord through his Exaltation. The passage therefore represents not an Exaltation Christology, as the first interpretation concludes, but a Humiliation–Exaltation rhythm which incorporates his divine pre-existence as a kind of Prologue to heighten the contrast. The divine descent into human existence only accentuates and does not detract from the humility of his earthly condition. This close link between Humiliation and Exaltation heightened or steepened by a prior act of divine descent is a constant theme of christologies from the side of God.

Of these two interpretations, with some hesitation, I accept the second as a further elucidation by Paul of the theme of pre-existence. The Adam imagery, surprisingly applied to the pre-incarnate Christ, is a link with his earlier Christology and the full humanity is by no means underestimated.

The Epistle to the Hebrews offers a unique combination of the theme of pre-existence and the full humanity of Jesus united by the concept of Christ as the Eternal High Priest. Scholars are not agreed about the theological background of the author, but there is much to be said in favour of the view that he sets the Hebrew and Christian realities against the background of the Platonic contrast between the temporal and the eternal. In the main the Pauline contrast between the two Ages becomes a doctrine of two Worlds. Philo had already interpreted the Old Testament on similar lines, and parallels to Philonic thought and language in the epistle are not negligible. Philo had, for example, interpreted the High Priest of the Old Testament as the Logos.

The opening verses contain a strong statement about pre-

existence. Through his Son God made the worlds. This recalls
the Wisdom theme of Colossians as well as Philo's statements
about the Logos. The following phrases, 'the effulgence of his
glory' and 'the express image of his substance', are remarkable
on any showing. The first derives from the book of Wisdom
but the word 'effulgence' can bear either an active or a passive
meaning. It could denote either the clear shining of God's
glory, an act from the side of God, or the (passive) reflection of
that glory mirrored in some lesser being. Its use in the book of
Wisdom and the unanimous interpretation of the Greek fathers
support the active and the stronger sense. In the balancing
phrase, 'express image' conveys the idea of the imprint of a
seal. Again it can be used in two senses, the act of impressing
the seal or the impression passively received by the wax. The
word 'substance' (*hypostasis*), also used of Wisdom in the
author's source, gives a more consciously philosophical turn to
the passage. While 'glory' is distinctively Hebrew, *hypostasis*
is distinctively Greek. Both are ways of expressing the inner
being of God himself. The active interpretation in both phrases
is supported both by their application in the sources to the
Wisdom and the Logos and by the use which the writer makes
of them to clarify the relation of the pre-incarnate Christ to
Creation and Revelation. The weaker interpretation which
explains both words from the image of God in Genesis hardly
measures up to the content of the passage. Other lesser
pointers to the meaning of pre-existence occur elsewhere in the
Epistle. In a comment on Ps. 8.5 Jesus is described as 'one who
for a short while was made lower than the angels, but now is
crowned with glory and honour' (Heb. 2.9, where the exegesis
is disputed), 'Son though he was, yet he learnt obedience
through the things which he suffered' (Heb. 5.8) and 'Jesus
Christ the same yesterday, today and for ever' (Heb. 13.8).
They furnish at best supporting evidence for the clearer
language of the Prologue.

   Yet no Epistle emphasises so radically the humanity of
Christ. He was 'tempted in all points like ourselves, yet
without sin' (Heb. 4.15). He was perfected and learned
obedience through his sufferings' (Heb. 5.8). There is an
unmistakable echo of Gethsemane, 'in the days of his flesh he

offered up prayers and supplications with strong crying and tears to him who was able to save him from death and was heard for his godly fear' (Heb. 5.7–8). He is the pioneer or file-leader of salvation, a title which recalls the early sermons of Acts (Heb. 2.10 and 12.2; cf. Acts 3.15 and 5.31). Robinson even claims to find a number of Adoptionist-sounding expressions in the epistle.

How then did the author come to pass so easily from one aspect of Christology to the other? The answer may lie in his concept of the High Priesthood of Christ. The contrast between the heavenly sacrifice and altar with which Christians are concerned and the earthly sacrifices offered at Jerusalem by temporary and mortal Jewish high priests is central to his argument. There is now a new order of priesthood, not according to Aaron (for which Jesus was not qualified humanly) but according to Melchizedek, whom the author describes, in an allusion to his sudden and unprepared appearance in Gen. 14, as 'without father, without mother, without genealogy, having neither beginning of days nor end of life' (Heb. 7.3). The strong language of pre-existence in the opening verses links up easily with this concept of priesthood. Aaronic priests are born, live and die. The Son of God abideth a priest continually. The Eternal Priesthood requires a pre-existent as well as a post-incarnate Person. Yet it is also a qualification for priesthood that the priest should be at all points like those whom he serves. 'Every high priest, being taken from among men, is appointed for men in things pertaining to God ... who can bear gently with the ignorant and erring, for that he himself also is compassed with infirmity' (Heb. 5.1–2). Thus with the sole exception of sin the full humanity of Jesus, our eternal high priest, is equally vital.

The author therefore provides a link concept of great range and power. This seems a step ahead of Paul who explores the concept of pre-existence without losing his theological grip on the humanity of Christ. Both use the language associated with the Word and the Wisdom without explicitly identifying the pre-incarnate Lord either with the Wisdom or the Word.

The final step was taken in the Prologue to the Fourth Gospel, where the pre-incarnate Lord is identified with the

Logos who is God and in relation to God. This twofold description probably reflects the aim of the Prologue to commend the gospel to two types of reader. The term Logos had currency both to Jew and to Greek but it had a different intellectual content in the two potential markets. For a Jew the Word was virtually a synonym for God speaking; while for many Greeks the Logos served as a link between the absolute and transcendent God and the contingent and relative universe. In the opening words of the Prologue each would find something familiar to their way of thinking combined with something strange. Both however presented possible points of entry into the gospel of the Incarnation.

But the real point of the Prologue comes not in the intriguing combination of Jewish and Greek ideas in the first verse but in the Christian application 'The Word was made flesh' (John 1.14). This was the new fact for which neither Jew nor Greek had needed to make theological provision. For the Greek this was a shocking paradox since for him the Logos and flesh were incompatibles which could not conceivably be united. For the Jew the paradox took a different form. The scandal came elsewhere—not in a divine coming but in the person in whom, as Christians claimed, his expectations had been fulfilled.

The remainder of the gospel works out the paradox of the Prologue on the basis of the existing gospel tradition. Here the author shows himself well able to live on both sides of the paradox at once. There is much force in Robinson's claim (*The Human Face of God*, pp. 169–79) that the story in the Fourth Gospel develops on two levels. We may call them the Word level and the flesh level respectively. The former has the priority but the latter is far from being ignored.

The humanity of Jesus is not disguised. He is weary (John 4.6) and thirsty (John 4.7; 19.28) and weeps for his friends (John 11.35). The Jewish view of Jesus as a Sabbath breaker (John 5.16); a potential revolutionary (John 7.12); an unlettered man (John 7.15); a sinner and evil-doer (John 9.24; 18.30) who makes blasphemous claims (John 10.33) is plainly set out. He is subject to arrest, imprisonment and death.

Yet the Word level is equally pronounced. He works

according to a divine timetable which is independent of human considerations. 'Mine hour is not yet come' (John 2.4; cf. 7.6 and 7.30); 'the hour is come' (John 12.23; 13.1; 16.32; 17.1). His self-affirmations are frequent and open; not partial and indirect as in the synoptic gospels. The hinterland of divinity of the earlier tradition now becomes a foreground simultaneous with, and parallel to, his humanity. He knows what is in man and has no need that anyone should bear witness concerning man (John 2.25). Nowhere is this interpenetration of the two levels more striking than with regard to the Passion. It is 'my hour', 'the hour'. With a fine irony of double meaning it is the lifting up of Jesus (John 3.14; 8.28; 12.32; 12.34). It is the glorifying of Jesus (John 7.39; 11.4; 12.23; 17.4–5). Even the shrewd political counsel of Caiaphas, 'It is expedient that one man should die for the people' (John 11.50; cf. 18.14) becomes by Johannine irony a proclamation of the Passion. Throughout the narrative Jesus is always shown as in control of events. The Cry of Dereliction from the Cross can have no place in the Johannine presentation of the Passion. The last words from the Cross, 'It is finished' (John 19.30) is more than the final cry of a weary sufferer; it is also a shout of triumph. The climax of the gospel comes in the wondering words of Thomas, 'My Lord and my God' (John 20.28).

The two sides of the paradox are not simply juxtaposed; they interpenetrate each other. It is therefore unsatisfactory either with Käsemann to claim that the gospel presents a docetic Christ, basically divine and human only in semblance, or, with Robinson, to maintain that the evangelist depicts a purely human figure who is nevertheless God's man. The Johannine interpretation of the Word made flesh—divine yet also human; human yet also divine—is the high-water mark of New Testament Christology.

The New Testament therefore not only offers us the available material about Jesus, but also begins the task of exploring his significance in the light of the Resurrection. It represents a period of rapid development. The humanity of Jesus was the obvious starting point; though even within the record of his earthly life there are hints which point beyond the exclusively human. After the Resurrection he was acclaimed as Lord, and therefore the object of worship as well as the subject of obedience. This was soon reinforced by the concept of pre-existence as a corollary of his impact after the Resurrection. This is more than a way of expressing his 'importance' for the Church, but implies a mode of existence no less personal than his presence in and with the Church. It was expounded with the aid of language and ideas associated with the Word and the Wisdom. The final step, taken by the Fourth Evangelist, the explicit identification of the pre-existent Christ with the Logos and his description as God and in relation to God, are no unprepared developments; but bring into focus material more lightly sketched elsewhere. Even the words of Thomas draw out the implications of the language of Phil. 2.6; Tit. 2.13 and possibly Rom. 9.5. There is abundant evidence for a duality of standpoint with regard to Christ, but little to support the view that his pre-existence and his humanity were, or were felt to be, incompatible with each other. The New Testament insights into Christ operate on the level of titles, images and concepts and the unity of its witness is enriched rather than weakened by the diversity of its interpretations. Later Christology will take over these insights and try to weave them together into a more formal pattern with the help of different conceptual tools and theological equipment.

3 The classical statement

FOR the early Church, the New Testament explorations towards a Christology were normative; but the attempt was made to give the doctrine a fuller and more rounded form, both for the sake of greater clarity and against oversimplifications which were regarded as inadequate or misleading. The fathers were at least as much biblical as philosophical theologians and their exegesis of the principal biblical passages is therefore often a reliable guide to, if not also the real starting-point of, their doctrinal concerns. They were also devout Christian men for whom the experience of being redeemed by Christ served as a doctrinal 'control' for their Christology. No doctrine of the Person of Christ could serve which failed to provide adequately for the divine conditions of Redemption. The link between Christology and the Eucharist became from time to time a leading case in doctrinal discussions. With so much at stake it was regrettable, but probably inevitable, that in the fourth and fifth centuries Christology became a battleground in which political and ecclesiastical rivalries played an important part. Yet solid doctrinal results were achieved and the lines of a classical statement of the doctrine ultimately achieved.

The intellectual equipment with which the Church faced its new task was drawn from Greek philosophy. This formed a common environment between the Church and its secular contemporaries. Without losing some of their distinctive features the older independent systems were tending to grow together. The use of Greek philosophy as a tool for Christian theology had elements both of loss and gain. The biblical preference for images was more open and flexible than the use of logical and metaphysical concepts which nevertheless were capable of providing a more stable and coherent framework.

Doctrinal precision therefore became the principal aim of the
period. Again the biblical dynamism fitted less easily into the
more static categories of contemporary philosophy. There was
some tension between the 'God who acts' of revelation and the
'God who is' of Greek philosophy. Thus Creation, which was a
fixed point for the theologian, presented a continual problem
for the philosopher. At times the theologian had to fight hard
to preserve the biblical insights within the new framework.
Normally however it was the intellectual scaffolding which
was adapted to this new purpose, and not the biblical realities
which gave way or were reduced to fit the new tools which
were being employed.

Three aspects of this tension are important for our purpose
here. In the Platonism of the period, the transcendent self-
existence of God was described by means of negative
metaphysical adjectives to affirm his freedom from the
limitations of time and space and other conditions of
creaturely existence. God is impassible (incapable of suffering),
immutable (not subject to change or alteration) and
incomprehensible (incapable of being grasped completely by
the human mind). While the theologian could fill these
concepts with positive content as pointers to the perfection of
God, he sometimes had to fight hard to preserve the ethical
dynamism of his biblical insights. While this whole framework
lent metaphysical stability to the doctrine of God, it
emphasised the ontological implications of deity rather than
the character and activity of the living God.

The technical terms used in the theology of the early Church
in the interests of doctrinal clarity were mainly derived from
Greek logic. They were originally used in the formulation of
the doctrine of the Trinity, and their application to Christology
was in some respects experimental, so that we cannot expect
them to be used in precisely the same way by all theologians.
Four words are of special interest. *Ousia* (substance) was used
at the Council of Nicaea in AD 325 to express the unity of
being between the Father and the Son or Logos. It could be
interpreted either as solidarity of being or identity of nature.
Hypostasis, originally identical with *ousia* in meaning, later
found its own level to designate the three Persons of the

Trinity. It had a note of concrete actuality, which made it particularly suitable to express that wherein in the Godhead was three. It was perhaps the word closest in meaning to our modern concept of personality. *Phusis* or nature represented the totality of attributes or qualities needed to describe a particular person or thing and to mark it off from members of another logical class. *Prosopon* (in Latin *persona*) had a more popular history but came to denote the person as seen from the outside. These are only rough and provisional definitions and would need much discussion and some qualification before they could be regarded as completely satisfactory. They formed however the best available apparatus used by the fathers to explore the double solidarity of the incarnate Lord with the Father and with ourselves, the unity of his Person and the characteristics both divine and human which were inalienably his.

In one vital area Greek philosophy failed to provide decisive help to the theologian. The humanity of Christ involves the prior question of the nature and structure of man. In this period, as for many later centuries, psychology was a branch not of science but of philosophy. It regarded man as having either a twofold (bipartite) or a threefold (tripartite) structure. The Platonist tradition worked with a threefold pattern of spirit (or mind), soul, and body while Aristotelians adopted a simpler twofold pattern of soul and body. The distinction may be little more than a matter of labelling. Here the Bible gave no clear guidance. The Old Testament works with a soul-body framework and the Spirit is always regarded as a special divine intervention in human life. In the New Testament there are a few tripartite passages (1 Thess. 5.23; Heb. 4.12) but its teaching about the structure of man usually remains within Old Testament limits. A second difference between the two philosophical schools had an important but less direct bearing upon Christology. For Platonism the universal (for example, Humanity) was philosophically more important than the particular human beings who exemplify and embody it. It had a prior and independent existence of its own. Aristotle however always started from the existence of individual particulars and regarded the universal merely as a convenient logical sorting device which made it possible to classify together similar or identical groups of objects. 'Humanity' therefore had no existence apart from the human individuals who could collectively be so described. This difference of emphasis had some bearing on the status of the humanity of Christ. For one main tradition it could be adequately described as 'humanity', for the other the description 'man' or 'the man' was an irreducible minimum requirement. Both intended to assert a real humanity but the implications of this claim were not identical.

It is at first sight surprising that the doctrine of the Trinity and not Christology was at the head of the Church's agenda. The reason however is fairly simple. The claim of Christianity to remain a monotheistic religion seemed to be set at risk by its affirmations about Christ and (somewhat later) the Holy Spirit. Both Jew and Greek were quick to point out this seemingly fatal inconsistency. The answer 'We are still monotheists, although we are Trinitarians' was not achieved in a day. The concept of an expanded monotheism which did not imply an exploded or abandoned monotheism took some four centuries to formulate and clarify. But even though Christology was not the leading issue some progress was made during the period to explore the doctrine.

A new urgency was given to the task of Christology by the teaching of Arius and the rise of Arianism at the beginning of the fourth century. The main question at issue, the relation between the Father and the Son, was primarily Trinitarian but in the course of debate the Arians made skilful use of Christology.

While the biblical data stress the unity of the Father and the Son, Greek philosophy used the Logos concept as a kind of windbreak or shock-absorber between the absolute God and the relative, and therefore metaphysically discreditable, universe. Arius (c.250–336) and his followers developed the tendency to assign a lower or subordinate status to the Logos into a veritable doctrinal system. The Father alone was fully God in his own right. The Son had an intermediate status; 'a creature but not as one of the creatures'. He could be honorifically described as God but owed his existence to the will of the Father. He was not co-eternal with the Father since 'there was a time when he was not'. The Holy Spirit was assigned an even lower status and can be described as a creature's creature. It was against this logical but implausible system that the term *Homoousios* (of one substance with the Father) was introduced into the Creed of the Council of Nicaea.

To support their views the Arians appealed to Christology and used the facts of the gospels to the theological discredit of God the Logos. The incarnate Lord grew in wisdom and in favour with God and man (Luke 2.52). He was ignorant of the date of the Parousia or Second Coming (Mark 13.32). He experienced trouble of soul (Mark 14.34; John 12.27). He felt himself abandoned by his Father (Mark 15.34), suffered and died. These facts (which the Arians attributed directly to God the Logos) appeared to them to exclude the claim that he was God in his own right or in any significant sense. Christ suffered, and therefore the Logos was passible. His temptations and agony displayed the Logos as mutable or subject to change. His occasional ignorance made the Logos fallible. Some Arians even denied that he knew the Father. At these decisive points the Arians claimed that the data of the gospels excluded the claim that the Logos was fully God. The Arians seem to have lacked any interest in Redemption and therefore an important control on their Christology was missing. The result of their doctrine, a demigod appearing in the flesh, could hardly satisfy either the data of the New Testament or the conditions of the Redemption which Christ came to bring.

Of greater interest for our purpose are the reasons which made the Arian misapplication of Christology feasible. On the positive side part of the Logos concept was the idea of the *Logos Hegemōn* or the directive Logos applied by Christian theologians to his activity in Creation and even in the incarnate Lord. On the negative side the doctrine of a human soul in Christ, though sometimes canvassed, was by no means universally accepted, especially in the theological tradition within which Arianism arose. Of course to argue directly from the Incarnation to the Trinity in the Arian manner was an illicit procedure. It telescoped two dimensions to the confusion of both. This fundamental criticism can be simply illustrated. Take the shape of a capital T. The horizontal crossbar may be taken to represent the Trinity while the vertical stroke may be deemed to depict the Incarnation. It is theologically impossible to 'feed back' without qualification what is true of the Incarnation into the doctrine of the Trinity. The Arians argued as follows: 'Whatever is stated of the incarnate Lord in the gospels must be ascribed directly and without reserve to the Logos. The incarnate Lord experienced growth, temptation, trouble of spirit, suffered and died. Therefore the Logos is passible and mutable and cannot be fully God.'

It was easy to see that the Arian position could not be regarded as a reliable interpretation of the Christian tradition. In the current state of Christology it was less easy to provide a satisfactory answer. Two sharply contrasted reactions which indicate the emergence of two rival christologies may be cited here.

The first is found in the fragments of Eustathius (bishop of Antioch *c.* 324–30). Starting from Col. 2.9, 'In him dwelt all the fulness of the Godhead bodily', he argues that what indwells is something different from that in which it dwells. He agrees with the Arians that the human experiences of the incarnate Lord are incompatible with the fulness of divinity which is by nature impassible and immutable. They must therefore be ascribed to the man, complete in soul and body, which the Godhead assumed and with which he clothed himself. In order both to preserve the full divinity of the Logos and yet to retain the human experiences at their full value, he is prepared, as it were, to change the subject from the Logos to the complete manhood. For him the human soul of Christ is no problem. It is assumed without question and forms the keystone of his argument.

A very different approach was adopted by Athanasius (*c.* 296–373). Whether he ever admitted explicitly the existence of a human soul in Christ is keenly disputed. He certainly never employs it in his long polemic against the Arians. He agrees with the Arians that the ultimate subject of the human experiences must be the directive Logos. Against them he argues that it is not the Logos in his own right as fully divine but the Logos as conditioned or qualified by the humanity who is the subject of the incarnate experiences. If we are to draw the proper inferences from the gospel statements about the Incarnation we must distinguish the times (*kairoi*) to which they refer. There are silences or reserves, appropriate to the incarnate Logos, which are inapplicable outside this particular context. Strictly they refer to the flesh or the body but, since the Logos has appropriated or made the body his own, they can be ascribed to the Logos. They must relate to him as, it seems, there is no other subject to which they can relate. But they cannot impair his impassibility or immutability as God, as the Arians claim. The tendency to reduce the compass of these experiences to passions of the flesh in order to accommodate them more easily to their divine subject was almost inevitable.

The text 'Jesus advanced in wisdom and stature and in favour with God and men' (Luke 2.52) was interpreted not of the human growth and progress of the boy Jesus but of the gradual self-disclosure of the Divine Logos. The ignorance of the date of the Second Coming (Mark 13.32, 'Of that day and hour knoweth no one . . . not even the Son but the Father') represents an accommodation of the all-knowing Logos to the conditions of the Incarnation; but it must also be taken in close connection with Acts 1.7, 'It is not given to you to know times and seasons which the Father hath set within his own authority', where there is no hint of ignorance on the part of the Ascending Lord. He could not fear death but must bear our passions in order to free us from them. The Logos could never be abandoned by the Father, and the Cry of Dereliction from the Cross must be balanced by the miracles associated with the Passion (the eclipse of the sun (Mark 15.33), the rending of the veil of the Temple (Mark 15.38) and the anticipated resurrection of Matt. 27.52. The death of Christ was simply the separation of the Logos from the body and it was the Logos who descended into Hades to perform 'the Harrowing of Hell'. In the exegesis of Athanasius there is a kind of flinching from the more poignantly human experiences in the gospels which borders on psychological docetism. Paradoxically the Arians were a more reliable guide to the human experiences of Christ than their most dedicated opponent!

These two approaches to the problem posed by the Arians, the one accepting and using to good effect the existence of a human soul in Christ, the other drawing a clear distinction between the Logos in his divine selfhood and the Logos conditioned by the fact of the Incarnation, but failing to apply this principle to the best advantage in exegesis, represent two sharply contrasted attitudes to Christology. Neither was completely unknown before the outbreak of Arianism and they soon developed into two traditions united in their opposition to Arianism but divergent from each other and increasingly in conflict, for reasons which were only partly theological. Broadly speaking, the one was linked with Alexandria, the other associated with Antioch. The rivalry of the two ancient Patriarchates of the East, and their struggle for the control of the upstart Patriarchate of Constantinople, added fuel to the flames. So far the battle had been waged largely in the field of exegesis but the attempt to convert their rival insights into full-scale systems led to even greater differences. The conflict in Christology was not simply concerned with words, though differences in their use of technical terms, deliberate as well as accidental misunderstandings, and 'the chasm of mutually omitted contexts' (G. L. Prestige, *Fathers and Heretics* p.326; SPCK, 1940) across which rivals glared at each other, all had their part to play. Neither tradition was unorthodox in itself though both were liable to produce equal and opposite exaggerations which were condemned as heretical.

In the outcome neither was capable by itself of providing for all that the Church found it necessary to affirm about Christ, though each made important contributions to the classical statement. Both traditions were firmly orthodox in their doctrine of the Trinity. Both worked within a common framework of the doctrine of God as absolute, impassible and immutable, though they disagreed on the nature of the divine involvement in Christ and its bearing upon the humanity of Christ. The root problem of Christology now becomes the relation between the divinity and humanity of Christ; the bond between them and the emphasis placed on each component nature.

The first, mainly but not exclusively associated with Alexandria, has been described as the Word–flesh tradition. Its Christology was firmly anchored in the Godhead both as its starting-point and as the organising principle within the incarnate Person. The Logos was the ultimate subject even of the incarnate experiences of Christ and its end product was a Logos-centred, Logos-preponderant Person. The emphasis lay upon the unity of the Person of Christ and the description of the tradition as Monist may therefore be equally apt. The Incarnation involved a divine descent into human life or, as Prestige describes it, a divine irruption or inbreaking. Its favourite proof text, indeed its biblical starting point, was John 1.14; and, though it could recognise that 'flesh' was a piece of biblical shorthand for 'man', it tended to regard the humanity as adjectival or instrumental to the divinity. Certainly the humanity of Christ lacked any independent value or significance. This could lead either to a theory of an incomplete humanity or, even after the doctrine of the human soul in Christ became widely accepted, an inability to use it to the best christological advantage. For the Monist tradition only a substantial or ontological bond of union could serve to explain the relation of God the Logos to his own flesh. Its doctrine of Redemption was equally centred in God. If the work of Christ was to avail for all men and be transmissible to all it must be centrally and vitally an act of God. In expositions of the doctrine of vicarious victory it is always the divine Logos who is the mighty victor on behalf of men. Nothing less could serve human need. The effect of Redemption was the deification of man. This was based on 2 Pet. 1.4: 'that we might become partakers of the divine nature', though this could be understood either ontologically in a strict and literal sense or mystically as the result of spiritual union with God through Christ. In the Eucharist we receive the lifegiving flesh of the Logos. Otherwise the sacrament could not transmit to us divine life and power.

The second tradition, linked with the Patriarchate of Antioch, has been called the Word–man tradition; but since it emphasised the full co-presence of two simultaneous natures, Godhead and manhood, the label of Dualist may be equally appropriate. While not denying the involvement of God the Logos in the incarnate life it was chiefly concerned to provide adequate living space for the humanity of Christ which was more highly valued and more realistically conceived than in the rival tradition. The high doctrine of divine transcendence common to both schools was here carried almost to the point which would make the Incarnation itself impossible. This was however directed against a doctrine of substantial union which, in their view, would detract from the divinity of God the Logos and endanger his complete humanity. The Logos would be less than God if he were made the subject of the human experiences of Jesus and the manhood could not fail to be swamped, or at least gravely impaired, by so close a bond of union. The Incarnation then involved not a substantial union of the Logos with the flesh but a looser conjunction of the divine Logos with a complete humanity. In harmony with its generally Aristotelian outlook, this tradition preferred to speak in concrete terms of the 'man' or 'the assumed man' rather than more abstractly of 'manhood' or 'humanity'. Its favourite proof-text was Phil. 2.5–11, where 'being in the form of God' (verse 6) and 'taking the form of a servant' (verse 7) were taken as references to two simultaneous co-present natures within the incarnate Lord. While John 1.14 (The Logos became flesh) was not neglected, the qualifications made in the course of Dualist exegesis shows that they were not completely happy either about 'became' or 'flesh'.

Again, where the Monists pointed to two successive states of the Logos, pre-incarnate and incarnate, the Dualists started from the two simultaneous natures of the incarnate Lord. They accepted without question the human soul in Christ and knew better than their rivals what to do with it christologically. It was the proper subject of the human experiences and existed side by side with the Logos within the incarnate Person. The human will, no less than the human soul of Christ, was important for christological as well as redemptive reasons. Indeed one main objection to any theory of substantial union was that it replaced a voluntary conjunction by a mechanical or involuntary union. Their opponents rejoined with the charge that Dualists merely maintained a relational or accidental union. While later in the period the Dualists tried to fit their christology into an ontological mould, their use of technical terms was so hesitant and tentative as to suggest that this was not their natural idiom. Their exegesis of the gospels displays an admirable realism and it is broadly true that they found themselves more at home with the synoptic than the Johannine presentation of Christ. In their doctrine of Redemption they assigned a real and sometimes a predominant place to the humanity of Christ. It is no accident that both in Christology and in their doctrine of Redemption the Epistle to the Hebrews was laid heavily under contribution. They avoided completely the language of deification as eliding the fundamental differences between God and man, and preferred to stress the ethical rather than the mystical aspects of Redemption. Ethics always keeps separate what mysticism tends to unite. The restoration of the human will through the saving obedience and victory of Christ was an important element in their doctrine of Redemption. If Christ (to use a vivid phrase of Nestorius) was to be 'our athlete' and the redemption which he brought was to speak to our condition, his victory must be his own with the assistance of the grace of God which is also available to us, and not an act of God the Logos. Since a relevant victory must imply the possibility of defeat, the text in Hebrews 'Tempted at all points as are, yet without sin' was of crucial importance for Dualists. A victory won divinely by God the Logos could only be a display of shadow-boxing. Their Monists rivals assumed that the incarnate Lord enjoyed a state of impossibility of sin (*non posse peccare*) as befitting a Logos-centred Person. Dualists, on the other hand, maintained the possibility of not sinning (*posse non peccare*) which through the grace of God and his own steadfastness became a saving actuality. At the Eucharist we receive the body and blood of the assumed man. There was a felt discontinuity of language in speaking of the life-giving flesh of the Logos.

In addition to the solidarity with the Father as God (the *homoousion* of the Nicene Creed) Dualists maintained an equal and simultaneous solidarity (*homoousion*) with ourselves. This double solidarity had the praiseworthy motive of making ample provision for the integrity and completeness

of the humanity of Christ, vital alike for christological and
redemptive reasons, and which they regarded their opponents
as setting at risk. For all its admirable realism their exegesis
was carried to the limit of dividing individual texts and
passages between God the Logos and the assumed man. For
example Theodore of Mopsuestia, a leading exegete of the
Dualist school, expounds some passages in the Fourth Gospel
as a dialogue between the two natures of Christ; examples
could easily be multiplied.

It can readily be seen that, if the Monist was always in
difficulties in assigning an adequate status to the manhood of
Christ, the main problem of the Dualist would be to provide a
satisfactory bond of union between the two natures which he
distinguished so clearly.

The Monist tradition was the first to move towards a
developed and integrated system. Despite his condemnation
for heresy this was largely the work of Apollinarius (*c.* 310–
90). The fragments of his writings disclose a thinker who
knows where he is going and why. A firm champion of the
Nicene cause, his uncompromising opposition to Dualism as
he understood it gave rise to a christology which bore an
uncomfortable resemblance to Arianism.

The Incarnation, according to Apollinarius, is centrally a
descent of God the Logos into whatever of humanity it was
fitting that he should receive. Incarnation is condescension or
self-emptying (*sarkosis kenosis*) though he never elaborates
this theme. 'One Christ and he divine' might be a fair summary
of his aim in Christology. The directive Logos is central to his
thought. The end product is a 'living unity', a 'living
combination, organised round the Person of God the Logos'.
So far as we know, Apollinarius was the first theologian to cast
about for technical terms to express this unity. In Christ there
is one activity, one nature (*phusis*), one *hypostasis* and one
prosopon. What distinction, if any, he drew between these
terms is uncertain in the absence of a supporting context in the
surviving fragments. It is possible that for him the accent fell
on the numeral 'one' rather than on the terms which follow it.
His most fatal legacy to Monist christology was the formula
'one incarnate nature of God the Logos' which came down to

later Monist christologians with the false authority of Athanasius, owing to the literary 'smuggling' in which his followers engaged after his condemnation. Recent research has however revealed a more dynamic, almost a vitalistic, thrust to his thought. Zoological analogies abound in his fragments and perhaps even *phusis* may represent a 'growing point' or organising principle within the incarnate Lord rather than the logical counter which it later became.

His quest for explanations had however more disquieting results. He can use the language of mixture or composition. As the mediator between God and man Christ is a whole of parts neither fully man nor God alone. The models which he uses to clarify his meaning: a mule half horse, half ass; or the colour grey which is a mixture of black and white, are hardly encouraging. In the light of his principle that 'two complete entities cannot form one' it becomes even more disquieting. It was gradually outgrown after his death and Cyril expressly excludes it.

The acid test of the success or failure of Apollinarius lay in his treatment of the humanity of Christ. The positive principle of the directive Logos and his negative inability to see how 'the unconquerable soul of the Logos' could be united to our own 'which is a prey to filthy imaginings' led him to liquidate the human soul (*nous*) of Christ. The extent of this deprivation depends in part upon the psychology which he adopted. Some fragments suggest a twofold structure but in others he adopts a threefold pattern. As early as the beginning of the fifth century it was suggested that his move from an earlier 'soul–body' formula to a later 'spirit–soul–body' classification was a desperate attempt to 'undergird the ship'. But in any case, if the governing principle in man was omitted, whatever else was present could only be a marginal matter. This denial of the human soul in Christ was the direct cause of his condemnation and it served as a warning to later Monist thinkers that continued neglect of this doctrine would imperil the success of their enterprise.

This christological weakness had devastating effects on his doctrine of Redemption. His definition 'incarnation is sanctification' (*sarkosis hagiasmos*) indicates that he was alive to the importance of the redemptive 'control' on Christology. He can use the argument effectively against the position of his Dualist opponents as he understood it. 'An inspired man cannot be the Saviour of the world.' 'The death of a man cannot annul death.' But whatever else of humanity Apollinarius believed the Logos to have assumed, the *nous* or directive principle was missing. This is no marginal matter since Apollinarius clearly believed that the *nous* and not the body was the seat of sin. The contemporary Cappadocian Fathers put their finger on the nerve of the problem. Gregory of Nazianzus makes the terse comment 'Not assumed, not redeemed'; while his namesake of Nyssa, writing against Arian opponents, excludes Apollinarianism as well: 'The Good Shepherd carried home on his shoulders not a fleece but a whole sheep.'

Apollinarius himself realised his problem and tries to meet it with the point that we are redeemed through our reception of the lifegiving flesh of the Logos. This clear allusion to the Eucharist is no doubt part of the truth but he never explains how it can completely meet his difficulty. The idea of redemption by deification, clearly expressed in one of the fragments, may have concealed for him the true dimensions of the problem. The strength of Apollinarius lies in his firm grasp of the divine involvement in the Incarnation. His fatal weakness lay in his defective sense of the place of the humanity both in Christology and Redemption. Apollinarianism remains a brilliant failure and the Monist christologian would need to take further steps if he were to commend his tradition to the mind of the Church.

Cyril of Alexandria (d. 444) gave to this tradition a more complete and systematic form. He was however a man of moods whose thought varies in balance and emphasis with the controversies in which he was engaged and the situation in which he found himself. His earliest writings against the Arians mark no considerable advance on the apologetic of Athanasius. References to the human soul of Christ are scanty and no effective use is made of the concept. Even after the outbreak of the Nestorian controversy the intransigent mood in which he wrote against Nestorius himself differs widely from the conciliatory tones in which he approached the moderate Dualists who showed themselves prepared to abandon their lost leader. If his essential convictions remained unchanged, the place which he was prepared to assign to the humanity of Christ altered as the heat went out of the controversy and efforts towards reconciliation were made.

He is aware of the need to avoid Apollinarianism and of the charge made by his opponents that he was simply an Apollinarian in disguise. He mentions the human soul of Christ frequently enough, though on Dualist standards he fails to make effective use of it in his christology. He explicitly rejects the language of confusion or mixture. Modern opinions of his christology range from a corrected Apollinarianism to the virtually Chalcedonian. The significance of this divergence will become apparent as we proceed.

Both as a representative of his own tradition and through his opposition to the Dualist Nestorius, his starting-point is the Logos-centred unity of the Person of Christ. He speaks characteristically of the Twofold Generation of God the Logos, eternally begotten by the Father and born in time of the Blessed Virgin. He quotes Heb. 7.3: 'without mother, without father', as a proof text. Even within the Incarnation 'what he (the Logos) was, he remained; what he was not, he assumed'. The Logos was one and the same both within and outside his incarnation without alteration or change. It was therefore wholly natural for him to describe the Blessed Virgin as the Mother of God (*Theotokos*), the title from which his controversy with Nestorius took its origin. For Cyril this was primarily designed to safeguard the full divinity of the Logos even within the Incarnation. Like Apollinarius he can describe the act of becoming incarnate as *kenosis* or condescension. It is a voluntary *kenosis* arising from an act of will on the part of the Logos.

But Cyril goes further and explores the implications of this act of condescension. It is a veiling (*krupsis*) of the glory of God the Logos to make it bearable to men. It implies addition (*proslepsis*) by means of the assumption of the limiting conditions of the humanity. More significant is the apparently contradictory description of *kenosis* as reduction of compass (*meiosis*) whereby the Logos allows the measures (*metra*) or proportions (*logoi*) of the humanity to prevail over himself. It may be doubted however whether Cyril exhausts the possibilities of this fruitful idea. He expresses the relation between the Logos and his human experiences by the phrase 'the impassible Logos suffered in the possible flesh' or in paradoxical shorthand 'he suffered impassibly' (*apathōs epathen*). This roused the ire of his Dualist opponents who regarded the phrase as playing with words. It was described as 'a ridiculous quibble' or compared in a homely metaphor to children playing sandcastles, building up and then knocking down. The two words cancel each other out. On the ignorance of Christ Cyril comments 'He usefully pretended not to know.' It is a question of an ignorance feigned for a good purpose, as if a teacher replied to a question 'I dont know' when he really meant 'You are not ready to receive the answer.' An opponent robustly comments 'Then the Truth tells a lie.' Cyril's aim is to preserve the divine status and dignity of the Logos even during the Incarnation. His success in using his acceptance of the human soul of Christ or his explanation of *kenosis* as reduction of compass to maximum advantage is more doubtful.

To safeguard the unity of the Person of Christ a substantial or ontological bond of union alone can suffice. Relying on the formula 'One incarnate nature (*phusis*) of God the Logos', which he borrowed from Apollinarius by mistake, he adopts a theory of natural union. He finds an appropriate model in the relation of soul and body out of which a complete man is constructed. Whatever the extent of the humanity, it is reduced by the participle 'incarnate' to a subordinate position. Cyril is not much given to the exact definition of his technical terms. Sometimes 'nature' seems to denote the sum of the qualities needed to answer the question 'what kind of a thing is present?' In this sense it is used in his preferred formula that the incarnate Lord is formed 'out of two natures'. His divinity and humanity are two entities, like the soul and the body in man, from which he is constructed. After the union they are only discernible under analysis or 'by abstraction alone'. But when he is speaking most strictly, it is only applied to God the Logos and here it seems to bear the meaning of a subject or a person metaphysically conceived. Sometimes he replaces *phusis* by *hypostasis* in his favourite formula with no very clear difference of meaning. The distinction, if any, is purely logical. *Hypostasis* might possibly round off *phusis* by adding the note of concrete actuality. At any rate his contemporary opponents failed to discover any important difference in sense between his two formulae. Yet, whatever his use of technical terms, he never failed to accuse his Dualist opponents of teaching a purely relational bond of union in Christ. Only a natural or hypostatic union could provide adequately for the divine involvement implied in the Incarnation.

His doctrines of Redemption and the Eucharist follow the lines customary to his tradition. He finds the focus of Christ's redeeming work in his divinity, and employs the language of deification to express its result. The Eucharist conveys to us the lifegiving flesh of the Logos.

Meanwhile the Dualist tradition underwent a parallel development, against the double threat of Arianism and Apollinarianism. Its leading theologian, Theodore of Mopsuestia (*c.* 350–428), was condemned long after his death as the precursor of Nestorius. In the Syrian Church he was described as the Interpreter and it is not surprising that his biblical commentaries are of special importance as evidence for his views. Yet it is also clear that he had a firm grasp of the main fields of theology. While Christology is the focus of his thinking he was not simply or narrowly a christologian. It will therefore be necessary to cast our net rather widely before addressing ourselves directly to his christology.

Theodore accepts without questions the high doctrine of divine transcendence common to both traditions. But he seems to hold an equally high doctrine of man. United to the visible world by his body and to the invisible world by his soul, man was created by God to be the cementing bond of the universe, a creature in whom God could behold the world as a whole. In the somewhat quaint expression of a German historian of doctrine, man according to Theodore was a 'cosmical god'. Theodore speaks with more than one voice on the Fall and its effects. While man still needs Redemption his plight is never described in as black terms as in the West. Even death is sometimes described not as the punishment for sin but as his natural condition. He remains a fit subject of an incarnation.

In his view of salvation history he has a deeper sense of eschatology than most Greek fathers. He returns to the Adam–Christ parallelism of Paul not only to stress the vital importance of the humanity, but also as the springboard for his characteristic doctrine of the two Ages or Conditions (*katastases*). The second Age was introduced but not consummated by the redeeming work of Christ. There is a 'Not Yet' as well as an 'Already' about our Redemption. The immortality, immutability and incorruptibility implicitly promised in the gospel will be ours only at the consummation of all things in Christ. Of this new Order Christ as man is the first-fruits; we enter it, but only as a pledge or a promise through participation in him. By Baptism we begin to share in the death and resurrection of Christ but the sacrament also points forward to its future fulfilment. At the Eucharist we receive the body and blood of the assumed man as our continuing food but we also look forward to our final goal in Christ. There is an actual experience of grace through the sacraments but the achievement of the full blessings of eternal life, immortality, immutability and incorruptibility belongs to the future. There can be no question of present deification since this would anticipate what will be only be ours at the consummation. Theodore's term 'participation' enables us to approach God through Christ, and yet to retain a respectful distance from him. We are in no danger of being swamped by God the Logos nor is his essential divinity impaired by too close an association with us. The fruits of participation are to be found in ethical living for which both the operation of divine grace and the exercise of the human will are necessary. For Theodore grace and freedom are correlatives and not in opposition to each other. This wider framework, derived both from the biblical commentaries and the lectures given by Theodore to candidates for Baptism, does not read like a theology devised to support a christology which has been independently worked out but as a coherent approach to Christian theology as a whole.

Theodore's critique of Arianism and Apollinarianism strikes

immediately at the concept of the directive Logos. To make the Logos the sole directive principle of the incarnate Lord would not only be an affront to his transcendent divinity but would inevitably swamp his humanity. For Theodore the integrity of the humanity of Christ is just as important as the dignity of the divine Logos. It is as man that Christ triumphed over sin and death and therefore for redemptive as well as christological reasons he must have both a human soul and will. Whatever the divine involvement in the Incarnation, the place of a full humanity is too valuable to be jeopardised for a moment.

In the christology of Theodore the distinction between the two natures is sharply expressed and may even be his real starting-point. They differ as the Assumer and the Assumed, and masculine rather than neuter pronouns are used of both. The Dualist preference for concrete rather than abstract expressions is indicated by the use of 'the man' or the 'assumed man' rather than 'manhood'. This may be a turn of phrase or a trick of style, but it seems more probable that Theodore would have answered William Temple's test question for christologians: 'If the Logos were taken away from the incarnate Lord, what would be left?' with the reply: 'A complete man.' Yet the Logos, although not substantially related to the assumed man, is still deeply involved in the Incarnation. From the moment of the Virgin Birth there is a conjunction, described as 'continuous' or 'exact', between the two. Like ourselves, the assumed man needs and receives grace which is not inconsistent with the full and unimpeded exercise of his human will.

This conjunction is also described as indwelling and, in a long fragment from his work on the Incarnation, Theodore explains what is in his mind. He begins by bracketing his target. It cannot be by *ousia* (a substantial indwelling) or by activity. His aim here is not only to exclude the Monist type of ontological theory of union but also to distinguish the special character of the Incarnation from the general immanence of God in the universe. The description which he prefers is indwelling by good pleasure (*eudokia*). The word is taken from the Voice from Heaven at the Baptism of Jesus (Mark 1.11). He offers a more precise definition as 'the best and noblest will of God'. At first sight we are back at a mere union in activity. This is certainly the general area, but it is activity raised to its highest power. If all will is activity, all activity is not will. It is also the will of God and this safeguards the divine initiative. The speciality of the Incarnation is also provided by the adjectives 'best and noblest'. It represents the preferential activity of God at its highest power. Even so Theodore finds it necessary to add a further qualification. It is an indwelling 'as in a Son'. This, like the term *eudokia*, marks a return to the biblical sources. His intention is to provide fully for the uniqueness of the Incarnation, while safeguarding at every point the complete humanity of Christ. But his initial framework of conjunction and indwelling makes it difficult for him to offer a satisfactory bond of union between the divinity and the humanity. The question whether he is thinking of two persons in 'godly union and concord' would have horrified Theodore. So far he has given no convincing answer to the contrary.

Particularly in his doctrinal treatises on the Incarnation he uses a more technical phraseology: *phusis, hypostasis* and *prosopon;* though the state of the evidence makes it impossible to reach firm conclusions. It is clear that he maintained two natures; probable that he affirmed one *prosopon*; wholly uncertain whether he wrote of one or two *hypostases*. He therefore tried to give a solid ontological basis to his christology. What precisely it was and whether it succeeded in supplying a unitary subject in Christ on his Dualist premises is doubtful in the present state of the evidence.

A fresh stage in the development of the Dualist tradition is marked by Nestorius (d. *c.* 451). In his general theological position there is little which is not already found in Theodore. His christology has a sharper edge but a narrower perspective than that of his great predecessor. The main difference between the two men is that, while Theodore died in comparative peace in an obscure see in Cilicia, Nestorius, Patriarch of Constantinople, had the misfortune to come into collision with Cyril. The occasion, the use of the title *Theotokos*, or 'Mother of God' for the blessed Virgin, seems at first sight trivial. It had long been cherished at Alexandria but was suspect at Antioch, in both cases for christological reasons. On its introduction at Constantinople Nestorius was conciliatory but hardly welcoming. There is some force in a contemporary judgement that Nestorius 'made a bugbear of the *Theotokos*'. What was really at stake was the christological technique known as the *Communicatio idiomatum* whereby attributes or activities proper to one nature are seemingly attributed to the other because of the unity of Person who includes or possesses both. Thus Paul speaks of the crucifixion of 'the Lord of glory' (1 Cor. 2.8) and of the Second Man as being from heaven (1 Cor. 15.47). It can easily be seen that the title *Theotokos*, which brings together 'God' and 'being born', is a further example of this device. Cyril's tight Logos-centred christology provided ample justification for its use. With their sharp distinction between the two natures, Dualists found it more difficult to accept without considerable qualification. As the controversy developed, Nestorius found himself accused of a heresy which he never intended and repeatedly disowned, the doctrine of 'Two Sons' or a double personality in Christ. By that time however the controversy had developed into a full-scale confrontation between the two rival traditions.

The opinions of Nestorius are best known to us in a work, the 'Treatise of Heracleides', written, it seems, shortly before his death and recovered in a Syriac version early in the present century. The greater part of the book reviews historically and doctrinally the course of his conflict with Cyril. It represents a piece of polemical Christology directed against Cyrilline and similar views. His critique of the doctrines of natural and hypostatic union is incisive and often repeated. It results in a necessary and mechanical union of incomplete natures which can provide neither for the completeness of the natures nor the voluntary character of their union. He offers a rival ontology of the Person of Christ which is easier to disentangle than that of Theodore even if in some details its interpretation is still disputed. His doctrine presupposes the analysis of a concrete person or thing into *ousia* (substance), *phusis* (nature) and *prosopon* (external undivided appearance) to which at times he adds *hypostasis* as a kind of logical 'joker' to reinforce the concreteness of his approach. Whether these terms are to be interpreted as items in a logical shopping list to be ticked off as present or absent or as different logical thrusts entering more or less deeply into a single reality is disputed; though both views can be defended. The *ousia* is not sharply distinguished from the *phusis* and Nestorius can pass from one to the other in particular passages without any break in the sense. *Ousia* is the final logical probe; the sorting of a person or thing into the appropriate class or logical genus. *Phusis* describes this in terms of the attributes or qualities which it involves. The *prosopon* 'makes known the *ousia*'. It is the external appearance of a person or thing considered as part of its reality and not in contrast to it. If recent discussion of the subject is correct, *prosopon* for Nestorius had a considerable 'property content' which in the case of persons might include even the will and the moral life. The intruding term *hypostasis*, sometimes associated with *phusis*, sometimes with *prosopon*, merely adds the note of concrete actuality to this rather abstract piece of logical analysis.

As applied to Christ this analysis gives the following results. There must be two *ousiai* in Christ since the double solidarity of the incarnate Lord with God and with ourselves was an important principle. Godhead and manhood cannot logically be classified together. There are two *phuseis* or natures since there are two sets of attributes befitting Godhead and manhood respectively and, unlike Monist thinkers, Nestorius prefers to distinguish them rather than to run them together. Without this degree of duality Nestorius could not have described the natures as 'self-sustaining'. So far he has given no logical account of the unity of Christ. In the fragments of his earlier work he had written explicitly enough of a single *prosopon* and by later standards this could not be faulted. But in this later and more elaborate analysis he recognises that each nature (if it is to be complete) must have its own *prosopon* and he therefore finds the unity in a mutuality or reciprocity of *prosopa*. Each nature uses the *prosopon* of the other. Clearly there must be some mutuality, otherwise no incarnation would be possible. What Cyril applies to the natures Nestorius reserves for the *prosopa* and thereby weakens his bond of union to an intolerable extent. Cyril's doctrine of natural union placed the mutuality in the wrong place and resulted in a mechanical union. Nestorius is so anxious to provide for a voluntary union of two complete natures that it is doubtful whether his own theory can support the weight of duality which it is asked to bear. The heresy of Nestorius lay not in an explicit affirmation of a double personality in Christ but in his failure to give a convincing account of the unity of Christ in which he evidently believed. Even his highly sophisticated theological analysis fails in the outcome to do what he asks of it. It cannot provide more than an additive subject (the one Christ = God the Logos + the assumed man). The Church will still have some distance to travel even on its own terminology before it can reach a satisfactory clarification of Christology.

Nestorius was condemned at the Council of Ephesus in 431 through a combination of forces which were only partly theological in character. Reconciliation was sorely needed, and by 433 the time was ripe for the attempt. By getting rid of Nestorius, Cyril had attained his main objective; and the moderate Dualists were prepared reluctantly to abandon Nestorius and to accept the title *Theotokos* with appropriate qualifications. The basis for agreement was the so-called Formula of Concord or Union-Symbol. It was a workmanlike document which marked no christological advance but indicated ground which could be held in common between the two rival traditions. No one (except Nestorius) had lost and all (except Nestorius) were to have prizes! Cyril had to defend himself against the charge made by his more extreme supporters of having sold the pass, and the extreme Dualists went off into schism.

It was one thing to arrange a cease-fire, another to make it stick. The closing stage of the controversy opened in 444 when Cyril's successor at Alexandria, Dioscurus, refused to be bound by it and the process of harrying Dualists was resumed. At Constantinople a new figure emerged of a very different type from Nestorius. Eutyches (*c.* 378–454) was a venerable archimandrite, the head of a monastery in the city, high in imperial favour and warmly supported by Dioscurus. Theologically he was a man of straw and his opinions are muddled and badly documented. He had an unlimited loyalty to Cyril but unfortunately did not understand him very well. He returned to the use of mixture language about the Incarnation which Cyril had excluded. He taught 'Two natures before the union, one nature after it', which indicates that he only assigned a paper or 'prescription' value to the humanity. He was reluctant to use the double solidarity (*homoousion*) formula but declared that the Mother, if not the Son, was solid with us. Ultimately, at the Home Synod of Constantinople at which he was condemned by his bishop Flavian, he declared himself willing to use the offending phrase. Events thereafter moved quickly. Eutyches appealed to all the major sees of Christendom (except Antioch) against his condemnation. he could be sure of the support of Dioscurus who probably welcomed the chance to interfere at Constantinople. The new Pope Leo (d. 461) was not only an experienced ecclesiastic but also a skilled theologian. His reply to Flavian, the Tome of Leo, is a balanced—though not an original—piece of Christology which represents the traditional teaching of the Western Church. It held the two sides of Christology in balance, confessing 'One Person (*persona*) in two natures (*substantiae*)' and making considerable use of the principle of the mutuality of attributes (*Communicatio idiomatum*). In the main it gave greater comfort to Nestorius in exile than probably to Cyril, had he lived to read it. The Emperor summoned yet another Council at Ephesus (449) which amply deserved Leo's bitter title, the Robber Council (*Latrocinium*). Dioscurus was in full control; Eutyches vindicated; the leading Dualist bishops extruded from their sees and the papal legates openly flouted. They were not even allowed to cause the Tome of Leo to be read.

Two years later, in 451, the Emperor died. The new empress Pulcheria had Dualist sympathies in Christology and in any case had scores of her own to settle with prominent supporters of Eutyches. A new Council was summoned to meet at Chalcedon to redress the balance of Ephesus. So far a settlement was fairly easily reached. Dioscurus and Eutyches were condemned and the Dualist bishops restored to their sees. But would the downfall of Eutyches lead to a demand for the rehabilitation of Nestorius? His recent death in exile made this less likely and the Eastern Dualists who might have supported it were in temporary disarray. They seemed content to leave the initiative in the capable hands of Leo who had his own cogent reasons for disliking the previous Council. The bulk of the Council still acknowledged the doctrinal leadership of Cyril and deeply distrusted what they understood to be the opinions of Nestorius.

During the Council itself the Illyrian bishops obtained an adjournment in order to satisfy themselves that the Tome of Leo did not conceal Nestorian tendencies. Leo himself would have been happy to see matters resolved by the redressing of former wrongs and the acceptance of his own Tome. From the imperial point of view however the time had come to attempt a new rapprochement between the two rival christological traditions in the East which could not be left for ever in uneasy tension, if not in active hostility. A renewed attempt to produce an agreed doctrinal statement on the lines of the Formula of Concord of 433 seemed most desirable and the Imperial Commissioners were instructed to ensure that this was achieved. Not without difficulty they secured the appointment of a Drafting Committee whose first draft was rejected and has not been preserved. The second attempt met with better success and was finally accepted by the Council under strong Imperial pressure.

The unusual step was taken by the Council of issuing a Recommended Reading List comprising the Tome of Leo and two letters of Cyril: his second and more moderate letter to Nestorius and his letter to John of Antioch containing the text of the Formula of Concord. The inclusion of the Tome of Leo was not only a tribute to the services rendered by the Pope to the whole Church but a recognition of the Western balance in Christology which had often been sadly lacking in the two main Eastern traditions. The list helps to explain the aims of the Council. It had no intention of rehabilitating Nestorius even by oversight, while the Cyrillines were warned to follow the lead of the conciliatory Cyril who had reached an accommodation with the moderate Dualists. In a sense it might be maintained that Cyril and Leo were the two most influential figures at the Council of Chalcedon. Neither however was present; Cyril had died some years earlier (444) and Leo, though represented by his legates, was excluded by papal protocol from attending a Council held outside Italy. Rightly or wrongly, the underlying assumption of the Council was the fundamental agreement of Cyril and Leo.

Like its predecessor of 433, the Chalcedonian Definition is not an original document. Its first paragraph follows closely the Formula of Concord but elsewhere phrases are also taken from the Tome of Leo, Cyril's second letter to Nestorius and other documents. Councils can arbitrate between the opinions of others. They can hardly be expected to produce systems of their own. Its intention was to exclude previous errors in Christology, Arianism, Apollinarianism, Nestorianism, and Eutychianism and, more positively, to delimit existing common ground in Christology and to set guidelines for future explorations.

The kernel of the document is contained in two paragraphs: the first concerned with the unity of the Person of Christ; the second with the duality of the natures, though there are dovetails from each into the thought of the other. The passage reads as follows:

> Following, then, the holy Fathers, we all with one voice teach that it should be confessed that our Lord Jesus Christ is one and the same Son, the same perfect in Godhead, the same perfect in manhood, truly God and truly man, the same consisting of a rational soul and a body: *homoousios* with the Father as to his Godhead, and the same *homoousios* with us as to his manhood; in all things like unto us, sin only excepted; begotten of the Father before the ages as to his Godhead, and in the last days, the same, for us and for our salvation, of Mary the Virgin *Theotokos* as to his manhood.

While Cyril had certainly accepted the substance of this paragraph by his endorsement of the Formula of Concord, characteristic Dualist touches are not lacking. 'Perfect in Godhead, perfect in manhood' he could accept as a description of the completeness of the two natures out of which the one Christ was composed, though the following phrase 'perfect

God and perfect man' was a characteristically Dualist
expression which they understood in terms of two co-present
natures. The double solidarity with the Father and with
ourselves which Eutyches had scrupled to use was more
difficult. Cyril himself had equivocated on the human
solidarity of Christ. The allusion to Hebrews which follows
was a favourite text for Dualists but left open the question of
the possibility of sin on the part of our Lord. The double
solidarity is well balanced by the typical Cyrilline doctrine of
the Twofold Generation of the Logos and the *Theotokos*
accepted with a qualification designed to make it acceptable to
Dualists. The repeated repetition of the 'same' and the explicit
statement 'one and the same Son' would be vital from Cyril's
point of view. Nestorius, as Monists understood his views, was
excluded by this emphasis on the unity of Person; Apollinarius
by the mention of a rational human soul in Christ; and
Eutyches by the express mention of the double solidarity.

The second paragraph is of greater significance:

> One and the same Christ, Son, Lord, Only-begotten, made
> known in two natures without confusion, without change,
> without division, without separation; the difference of the
> natures having been in no wise taken away by reason of the
> union, but rather the properties of each being preserved, and
> both concurring into one *prosopon* and one *hypostasis*—not
> parted or divided into two *prosopa* but one and the same
> Son and Only-begotten, the divine *Logos*, the Lord Jesus
> Christ.

While the paragraph is primarily concerned with the duality
of the natures it opens and ends with strong affirmations of
unity. The four negative adverbs are paired off against Monist
and Dualist exaggerations. 'Without confusion' is aimed at the
use by Eutyches of mixture language; 'without change'
directed against Arianism. 'Without division, without
separation' excludes Nestorius as currently interpreted. The
following phrases are both quotations, the first from Cyril's
second letter to Nestorius, the second from Western sources no
doubt through the agency of the Papal legates.

So far the four negative adverbs, none of which was original to or invented by the Council, had served as 'No Road' notices for tempting by-paths in Christology or 'marker-buoys' for future navigators between the Scylla of Eutyches and the Charybdis of Nestorius.

With regard to terminology more important advances were made. The clear affirmation of 'in two natures' marked a notable step forward from the ambiguous 'of two natures' of the Formula of Concord and still more from the 'out of two natures' favoured by Cyril. It represented both the Dualist preference and the formula traditional in the West. It is a reasonable conjecture, not unsupported by indirect evidence, that the first rejected draft marked no advance here. The starting-point of the Dualist tradition was secured for the future. The unity of the Person of Christ is described as one *prosopon* and one *hypostasis*. This is more significant than it appears at first sight. Against Cyril it distinguishes the use of *phusis* and *hypostasis*. The former must be used of that wherein Christ was twofold, the latter reserved for that wherein Christ was one. At last the widespread uncertainty whether there were two *hypostases* in Christ or only one was brought to an end. Against Nestorius the Definition insists upon one *prosopon* as the sole usage acceptable for the future. There must be no more talk about two *prosopa* or of a mutuality or reciprocity between them. Leo's formula 'one Person' (*persona*) was probably decisive here.

The significance of this important clarification in the use of terms extended even further. It conveyed implicit warnings to both the main Eastern christological traditions. The distinction between *phusis* and *hypostasis* reminded Monists that they could legitimately make room for a greater measure of duality at the level of the *phusis* without detriment to the unity in *hypostasis* while by the equation of *prosopon* and *hypostasis* Dualists were warned that they must provide a firmer and more solid bond of union than their struggles with the notion of an additive subject had hitherto supplied. The guidelines for a future Christology were laid down negatively by the four adverbs and positively by the new terminology.

For the immediate future the question was whether the

Definition was to be interpreted according to Cyril or Leo or Theodoret. Could the Monists take advantage of the considerable elements in their tradition which the Definition contained to produce a corrected Monism which could win the support of the whole Church? At first sight this seemed improbable since the first effect of the Council was the Monophysite Schism or the severance from the Church of those for whom the Cyrilline formula, 'One incarnate nature of God the Logos', was vital. This no doubt included many who thought with Eutyches but also a number of more moderate Monists who genuinely believed that the Faith was in danger. In the longer run however it was a formula of this type which came to prevail. Or could the Dualists take advantage of the many Dualist touches which the Definition contained to supply a Christology freed from the obscurities and overemphases of Theodore and Nestorius? For this they were unfavourably placed after the tragedy of Nestorius and the débacle of the years which followed the death of Cyril. Their leading contemporary theologian, Theodoret, (*c.* 393–458) though competent and discerning, lacked the originality required for the task. Leo had never wanted a new definition of faith and his own christology in the Tome advanced no further than the use of clear technical terms and a balanced statement of the ingredients of the problem. While his influence at Chalcedon was invaluable, at this period at least the West did not press christological inquiry as far as the East. In the long run however the official christologies both of East and West through the systems of John of Damascus and Thomas Aquinas resulted in a revised Monism.

Of late the Chalcedonian Definition has had a bad and not altogether deserved press. G. L. Prestige (*Fathers and Heretics*, p. 298) writes: 'The formula states admirably what Christ is not. On the constructive side it merely says with Nestorius that he is one perceptible figure, and with everybody except Nestorius that he is one objective reality or *hypostasis.*' Even on the constructive side this is not quite correct. It is untrue to the main aim of the document to delimit ground which could be held in common and misses completely the promise for the future which lay behind the precisions in terminology. In an early essay in *Foundations* (1910, p. 230) William Temple described it as the 'bankruptcy of Greek patristic theology' but this had a long and fruitful history after the Council. Tillich claims (cf. *Systematic Theology*, II, p. 167) that Nicaea and Chalcedon taken together preserved both the Christ-character and the Jesus-character of the event of Jesus as the Christ, but with very inadequate conceptual tools. In particular the term 'nature' is the basic inadequacy. When applied to man it is ambiguous; when applied to God it is wrong.

Certainly the fathers cannot be blamed for using the only conceptual tools available to them. The new terminology recommended at Chalcedon at least made it possible to distinguish with some accuracy that wherein Christ could be described as one and that wherein he was twofold. In the outcome *hypostasis* approximated to Person, understood ontologically as the ultimate subject of the incarnate life, while *phusis* or nature was understood as the totality of attributes which make up his humanity and divinity respectively. No doubt there are differences in the way in which nature can be predicated of God and man respectively. Nature is what God *is*; it is what man *has*. It is not clear that any alternative framework has been satisfactorily provided and in my opinion it is arguable whether Tillich has supplied a better formulation. From the time of Harnack onwards exception has been taken to the metaphysical framework in which the fathers sought to fit Christology together with other doctrines. It is a question of the nature and extent of the involvement of the Logos in the incarnate Person. Ontology seems the only framework solid and substantial enough to express the being of God and it is natural that it should be applied to the Person of Christ by those whose Christology starts from the side of God.

If however the opposite approach is adopted in christology, a starting-point from the side of man, there might seem to be a *prima facie* case for focusing the doctrine in some such concept as 'will'. Both approaches are in principle admissible for those who wish to maintain the double solidarity of our Lord with the Father and with ourselves. As we review each type in turn we shall need to ask which provides the richer and more satisfying christology.

A final objection, more often felt than explicitly stated, raises the question of the difference in texture between the Christ of the New Testament and of the Church's worship and the dry and abstract formulations of the early centuries. The difference however is not quite as absolute as might be thought. The gospels imply at least the beginnings of a christology while the fathers, as we have seen, make a substantial use of the gospels both in their exegesis and their christology. The closing statement of the Chalcedonian Definition which appeals both to the Creed and to the New Testament indicates that Chalcedon had no intention of cutting the painter from the roots of the Church's life. Admittedly there is a considerable difference between a photographic representation of Christ (even if this were possible) and the construction of a doctrine of his Person. What the fathers (and later christologians) were attempting was not a mere repetition of the biblical portraiture of Christ but the attempt to draw out the inferences in thought which best supported the biblical faith and the Church's experience.

The person of Christ in history and faith stands fast. Without it the enterprise of christology would never have been set in hand. Its various end-products cannot be regarded as treachery to the gospel or as substitutes for the Person but as elucidatory doctrines drawing out the implications of Christ against a particular background of thought. The bare bones of the doctrine are not the the bare bones of Christ himself. They are simply the theological construct intended to convey the meaning of the Person as adequately as possible. The Chalcedonian Definition still supplies the classical and most ecumenical statement of Christology. Many of us hold that in balance and perspective, if not also in terminology, it still provides the truest norm of Christological enquiry.

4   Christologies from the side of God

IN our discussion of recent christologies, it will be better to describe them as doctrines which start from the side of God and from the side of man respectively, for reasons which will become apparent as we proceed. The new terms correspond fairly closely to the Monist and Dualist traditions of the early Church.

As the christologies discussed in this chapter are in direct continuity with the 'corrected Monism' of the period after Chalcedon in the sense indicated in the previous chapter, it will facilitate comparison to sketch briefly and without detailed discussion the nature of the Christology which became dominant both in the East and the West.

The Council of Chalcedon had laid down that the incarnate Lord must henceforth be described as one person (*hypostasis* or *prosopon*) in two natures (*phusis*). This left two questions unresolved; some account of the way in which the Logos could be described as the ultimate subject of two disparate natures, and the content of the term *phusis* applied to the humanity.

The first question was the more difficult of the two. The manhood could not be described as having its own *hypostasis*; that would lead to two subjects in Christ or Nestorianism. To speak of the humanity as having no *hypostasis* at all would be Apollinarianism and leave it completely in the air. The solution which proved acceptable in the thought-climate of the time was that the Logos himself did double duty as the ultimate subject of both natures. Since in being God the Logos he included all that perfect humanity involved, this view was regarded as feasible. The humanity therefore could not be said to lack a *hypostasis* even though it had no independent *hypostasis* of its own. This idea of an included *hypostasis* was

60

called the *Enhypostasia*. It fell within Chalcedonian limits and commended itself to authoritative theologians both in the East and in the West such as John of Damascus (*c.* 675–749) and Thomas Aquinas (*c.* 1225–74). Given the intellectual apparatus of the period it was perfectly viable.

If the humanity of Christ lacked its own independent *hypostasis*, it included everything else, a human soul and will. The notion that the human soul and will formed part of his *phusis* without pointing also to a human *hypostasis* would have seemed strange to Nestorius. But for the classical Christology the centrality of God the Logos and the full measure of divine involvement in the Incarnation seemed to demand this largely logical sacrifice. The theory of the *Enhypostasia* is often described as a doctrine of the 'impersonal humanity'. This is an unhappy description for two reasons. It concentrates on what, in this view, Christ lacked (an independent human *hypostasis*), without reference to the complementary and more important truth that this missing element was supplied by the action of God the Logos. It is also misleading because much of what we should include in personality—a human soul and will—was described by the fathers under the head of 'nature'. Strictly the doctrine only relates to the logical subject of the humanity of Christ and does not imply any psychological deficiency in his assumed humanity.

The fathers were fortunate in having a conceptual framework in common with the best secular thought of the day. This has unfortunately long ceased to be the case and the changes which have occurred will need further discussion in the next chapter. But two points are significant here. The first is the changed status of psychology from a branch of philosophy to a science in its own right. So far we have not found a technical term which can be translated 'personality' in the modern sense. Personality has two aspects which at first sight appear contradictory. The first is self-subsistence, the irreducible 'Me-ness' of me and the 'You-ness' of you which is, or should be, impregnable. On the other hand an important ingredient in personality is capacity for fellowship. No man is an island and we usually measure the effectiveness of a personality by its ability to enter into full and many-sided relations with other people. Personality is not like the talent in the parable which was wrapped up and hidden in the ground; it must be given to the money-changers when it will receive its own with usury. The classical Christology used the term *hypostasis* and its Latin equivalents to describe the self-existence and concrete actuality of a personality. Its other aspect was defined in terms of relations and therefore regarded as accidental or attributive only, and not, as many modern psychologists would regard them as constituting a personality. The early concept of a Person was a logical and not a psychological term. It denoted the logical subject and, though this may cover part, it is certainly not the whole of the modern notion of personality. The term 'consciousness' which bulks so largely in modern discussions of personality played no part in the thought of the fathers.

The second change affects the doctrine of God. The fathers accepted a high doctrine of divine transcendence expressed by means of negative metaphysical adjectives like 'impassible' and 'immutable', though the two main christological traditions drew different inferences from them with regard to the Incarnation. The emphasis here has changed. It is not that the fathers argued wrongly on their premises, but they were laying down the logical preconditions of deity rather than pointing to the nature and character of the living God. Some later christologians have felt a tension between these two approaches and have tried to take action to escape from it.

The best modern presentation of the classical Christology is given by Karl Barth, the leading Reformed theologian and the author of the massive but unfinished *Church Dogmatics* (T. & T. Clark, 1935–62). His starting-point is the givenness of Revelation, not identical with the Bible, but of which the Bible is the only authoritative source-book. This premise ensures a more biblical presentation than the classical statements of the fifth and sixth centuries adopted. He is however fully proficient in the method and terminology of the classical period and reaches conclusions which are identical with the common orthodoxy of East and West, although by a different and in some respects a simpler route.

Barth's Christology occurs in two widely separated parts of the *Church Dogmatics* under *The doctrine of God* (I, i, pp.457–512; I, ii, pp.1–44) and *The Doctrine of Reconciliation* (Iv, i, pp.157–308; IV, ii, pp.1–154). We might expect a sharp distinction between the doctrines of the Person and Work of Christ but in fact some of his more technical discussions of the Person of Christ occur in his later discussions. There is a certain amount of repetition in his treatment of Christology and, while he realises that this is a somewhat unhandy procedure, he confesses that he has found it unavoidable.

The biblical witness is that Jesus Christ is the Lord, but he is also the Servant of God who proclaims and executes the work of his Father in Heaven. There is therefore both a unity and distinctness in his relation to the Father. The affirmation that Jesus is Lord leads directly to the divinity of Christ. This is not an inflated inference from the New Testament but its fundamental statement. He is God (*theos*), not simply divine (*theios*) for, whatever he is, he is antecedently. The conditions of Revelation cannot be satisfied either by the divinisation of a man or a mere appearance of God in the flesh. Adoptionism and Docetism are therefore both non-starters. He is neither a peak of history soaring into superhistory nor a sucker of superhistory reaching down into history. The metaphor here is botanical, of a shoot of a plant or a tree used for purposes of propagation. Neither a deified man nor a humanised God can serve our need. Only God can reveal God. Christ is not therefore 'all but God' (in the weaker sense of the word 'divine') nor 'somehow God' (performing some of the functions of God for us), but 'Very God' or truly God. Revelation and Redemption do not 'create' his deity; rather his deity 'creates' or is the precondition of both. God in himself precedes God for us, and even more, God in us (*Church Dogmatics*, I, i, pp.357–484).

So far Barth has merely been setting out the conditions of Revelation. He now makes the transition to the Incarnation. Here two principles are quite fundamental. The first is the freedom of God which springs directly from his Reformed insistence on the sovereignty of God. The Incarnation establishes the freedom of God to be our God just as the

outpouring of the Spirit affirms man's freedom for God. We
cannot therefore prove the necessity for the Incarnation on
general theological grounds alone. Its necessity arises from the
fact itself and not from anything outside of or prior to the fact.
His second principle is the centrality of Christ to Revelation,
even though for Barth the prime subject of Revelation is the
Triune God himself. Since Jesus Christ is the chief agent in
Revelation, the Incarnation becomes central.

He is the reality of Revelation; once for all, unique,
unrepeatable, and therefore God's Revelation for us, just as the
Spirit is God's Revelation in us. Christology is the
interpretation of the Christ in whom the reality of Revelation is
focused and centred. The fact must come first; the
interpretation second. The distinctive New Testament witness
to Christ can be expressed in two ways. 'The Word of God
becomes a man'; 'This man, Jesus Christ, was God's Word', or
'God's Son'. Barth has already distinguished the Synoptic
witness to Christ 'In *Jesus* we find God' from the Johannine
presentation 'We find God in Jesus'. The two are
complementaries, not contradictories (*op. cit.*, I, ii, pp.1–44).
Two points may be noted here. Throughout his work Barth
prefers to speak of Christ as the Word, whereas we have
chosen to speak uniformly of the Logos. Since the Word is the
translation of the Greek Logos in John 1.1 and 1.14 the
difference is more apparent than real. The meaning is identical.
Barth has already shown his preference for the phrase 'a man'
rather than simply 'man'. This is mainly due to his preference
for the concrete rather than the abstract. His precise meaning
and still more the implications of his use are found later in his
discussion.

He next approaches the central theme of Christology under
the form of an extended theological commentary on John 1.14.
While the text must be read as a whole if the true paradox of
the Incarnation is to be grasped, it nevertheless admits of
detailed analysis. '*The Word* became flesh.' The subject of the
Incarnation is the Word in his divine freedom; there is no
movement on the part of the creature. As subject, the Word
cannot become the predicate or object of any sentence of
which the subject is anything other than God himself. Despite

the fact that Barth can describe the 'flesh' as 'a man', it is only predicate and never subject. The Word is what he is apart from the flesh, but the flesh would not be flesh apart from the Word. To Temple's famous question 'If the Logos (the Word) were taken away from the incarnate Lord, what would be left?' Barth would reply 'Nothing at all' despite his description of the flesh as 'a man'. The true manhood cannot be regarded as a theoretically detachable man. This excludes any possibility of Jesus worship, whether of the Sacred Heart variety or the pietistic type. It also excludes any cult of the historical Jesus on the interesting ground that you cannot write the biography of a predicate. In this last phrase Barth rejects on theological grounds the attempt to reconstruct, from the gospel witness to Christ, the biography of a historical figure who is worshipful apart from his Resurrection and post-resurrection impact.

'The Word became *flesh*.' He became participant in human nature and existence. But since this cannot be real except in the concrete reality of one man, we must say that he became 'a man'. This does not mean that first there was a man and then the Son of God became that man, but that the Son of God assumed the possibility of becoming a man to himself, and actualised it when he became Jesus. The Word, while remaining all that he was before, became what he was not before, a man—this man—but *this* man. By this threefold repetition Barth is adding emphasis to his view of the concrete individuality of the humanity of Christ although it necessarily lacks an independent human *hypostasis*. The manhood assumed by the Word was full Adamic sinful humanity, liable to sin, yet without sin. For Barth the sinlessness (or more positively, the perfect obedience) of Christ is not in doubt, but anything further, like the impossibility of sinning, would involve a hidden danger of Docetism.

'The Word *became* flesh.' This 'becoming' is not an event which happened to the Word. Even his sufferings are the product of his will and his work. There is no action and reaction between the Word and his flesh. The one is active, the other passive. Hence the classical word 'assumption' is preferable to the language of 'becoming'. Nor does the Incarnation involve any change, transposition or admixture in the Word nor the production of any hybrid figure between God and man. The God-man is formed by the assumption of the flesh by the Word and results in a personal or hypostatic union. Nothing less will satisfy the conditions of the Incarnation. The result of this union can be described negatively as the *Anhypostasia* since the manhood does not possess its own *hypostasis* or positively as the *Enhypostasia* since the manhood is assumed by God the Word who serve as its *hypostasis*. This manhood, this man, is not autonomous or self-existent, for its reality, existence and being depends upon God acting through his Word unilaterally. What is being denied here is not what we call personality but autonomous or independent self-existence. For Barth the notion of an 'impersonal manhood' is far from being the correct interpretation of the doctrine.

At this point Barth introduces his discussion of the Virgin Birth. The Virgin Birth does not create the Incarnation. The mystery (of the Incarnation) does not rest upon the miracle (of the Virgin Birth); the miracle rests upon the mystery. Like its counterpart, the Empty Tomb, the Virgin Birth sets the boundaries of the mystery which lies between. Barth accepts the historical evidence for the Virgin Birth as sufficient, though of a different texture from the 'Crucified under Pontius Pilate'. It is a sign of which the Incarnation is the thing signified. It safeguards the divine initiative, God's sovereign freedom in word and deed. In the miracle this is expressed both positively and negatively. 'Born of the Virgin Mary' denies that the true man is a completely detachable man. 'Conceived of the Holy Spirit' affirms the true God. The Virgin Birth is wrongly understood as a piece of biological inquisitiveness. The action of the Holy Spirit represents the overshadowing of the divine love (*agapē*) without any taint of human passion (*erōs*) whatsoever. Barth here applies to the Virgin Birth the sharp distinction drawn by Bishop Anders Nygren, a Swedish Lutheran scholar, between human passion (*erōs*), a grasping, taking and possessing activity, and the love (*agapē*) of God which is always giving and outgoing in its relation to men. The absence of paternity in the Virgin Birth underlines the fact that the divine initiative in the birth of Christ is markedly and decisively different from a normal human birth which is always preceded by human intercourse. Such is not the manner in which the pre-existent Word entered the world.

The Incarnation then for Barth does not stand or fall with the miracle of the Virgin Birth; although for those who do not accept it or regard it as theologically dispensable the Incarnation must have a different theological texture. Christ is not the Son of God because he was 'conceived of the Holy Spirit, born of the Virgin Mary'; rather it is because he is the Son of God that we believe him to be Virgin-born. Barth then not only accepts the Virgin Birth as a historical fact but also knows what to do with it christologically (*op. cit.*, I, ii, pp. 122–202).

Barth returns to Christology in Volume 4 of the *Church Dogmatics*, subtitled *The Doctrine of Reconciliation*. His discussion falls into two parts, called (somewhat emotively) 'The Way of the Son of God into a Far Country' and 'the Homecoming of the Son of Man.' The first relates to Jesus Christ the Lord as the Servant, the second concerns Jesus Christ the Servant as the Lord. The first section contains Barth's criticism of Kenotic Christology, a movement in nineteenth-century Christology based on Phil. 2.7: 'He emptied himself' (in Greek *ekenōsen*) and claiming that in order to become incarnate the Eternal Son of God divested himself of some of his divine attributes and thereby ceased (according to Barth) to be 'wholly and unalterably God'. Some Kenotic views which may not be as damagingly exposed to this criticism as Barth thinks, will concern us later in this chapter.

'In him dwelt all the fulness of the Godhead bodily.' This biblical insight underlies fifth-century Christology and it continued unbroken until the emergence of Kenoticism in the last century. God is always God even in his humiliation. The intactness of the Word both inside and outside the flesh is the common theme of traditional orthodox Christology. Against Kenoticism Barth urges that, unless in Christ God, wholly and unalterably God, is involved, Reconciliation is left in thin air. The mystery of the Incarnation is far greater than Kenoticism supposes. True God has become True Man. Against Kenoticism Barth considers two alternative possibilities. We might regard the Incarnation as the ultimate paradox, God not only giving himself but giving himself away. This would convert the supreme mystery into the ultimate blasphemy. This represents Barth's implied comment on the Death of God movement, and with good reason! But another alternative is open; the Incarnation considered as an act of divine omnipotence in love, a divine fulness of power which, unlike an abstract or formal omnipotence, can assume the form of weakness and impotance. God, the same God—not another God, as Kenoticism presupposes—becomes God for us by an act of obedience wrought in the free omnipotence of God. It is a voluntary *kenosis*, a decision of love which nevertheless remains a decision of omnipotence.

Why did the Son of God become a Servant, or (in Anselm's question) *Cur Deus Homo*? Barth replies with the Bible and the Creeds, 'for us men and for our salvation'. He has already established that God in himself is always prior to 'God for us'. Now he lays down the further proposition that 'God for us' is always prior to 'God in us'. As our Saviour, the Word becomes our Brother, but he could not be our Saviour if he were not also our Judge. He executes the judgement of God upon us by taking it upon himself. In the vigorous phrase of a second-century father he is 'the judge who is judged and yet keeps silence'. He took our place as the judged and was judged in our place. All this he suffered before God and in obedience to God. The Resurrection is God's 'Yes' to the act of obedience of his Son. The new order which he initiates will find its completion and fulfilment in the Parousia or Second Coming of Christ (*op. cit.*, IV, i, pp.157–358).

If the section 'The Way of the Son of God into a Far Country' was devoted to the condescension of God, Barth's final discussion of Christology, 'The homecoming of the Son of Man' concerns the exaltation of man to God. The theology of the Cross (the high peak of the condescension of God) leads to a theology of glory the summit of the exaltation of man in and through Christ). Here Barth insists that Jesus Christ, true God and true man, is the essential precondition both of Christology and of the Atonement. The double solidarity with the Father and with ourselves is vital in both fields. His High Priesthood

as God is matched by his Royal office as man. Like us Jesus is
a true man; unlike us he is *the* true man. He is exactly the same
as we are, but quite different not merely quantitatively but also
qualitatively. It is not as if he were a man in whom there was
more of God than in us. In him there took place an exaltation
of the humanity which is both ours and his. God became *man*:
The Creator became a *creature*. From this point of view the
Incarnation is an event in world history. But also, *God* became
man. The *Creator* became a creature, and that is a unique
event.

Of this event God the Son is the active subject; man is
always the object or the predicate. 'Becoming' must always be
understood as 'Assuming'. The result is the Son of God made
Son of Man. The object of this assumption by the Word is
neither humanity, an abstract universal, nor a man in the sense
of one of many who existed. The former would lead to an
impersonal humanity, the latter to mere Adoptionism or a
duality of subjects in Christ (Nestorianism). The point of the
Enhypostasia is to exclude both these options. The subject of
Jesus Christ is the divine Word but the human essence or
nature is complete. Barth defends this position with the
observation that perfection relates to the nature or essence of a
thing and not to its *hypostasis*. The humanity of Christ can
therefore be said to be perfect despite the absence of its own
appropriate human *hypostasis*.

Finally he turns to the implications of the personal or
hypostatic union. The incarnate Lord exists not only as God
with the Father and the Holy Spirit, but in this act of human
history also as man, this man with concrete actuality. As a
man among men he is a human Thou, but he is also directly
the Thou of the eternal God. Barth now discusses some models
for this hypostatic union which have been proposed and finds
the least inadequate to be the nature of the Church. The
Church is incorporated into the humanity of Christ but it is
anhypostatic to the humanity of Christ. The Body of Christ
cannot exist for a moment without its Head but the proposition
cannot be reversed, any more than we can say that the flesh
'becomes' or assumes the Word.

The final steps in Barth's Christology are even more

technical but are needed to round off the picture. They relate to
the union of the two natures within the personal or hypostatic
union. In the one Christ the two natures human and divine are
united. What may be called a two-dimensional Christology
which involves a full double solidarity is inescapable. The
union in a single Person of Godhead and manhood, which by
definition cannot be so related, has actually taken place. This
has actually happened and must therefore find christological
expression. In the one subject Jesus Christ divine and human
are related but not made one and the same. He is both together
without the destruction of either. This is the point of the first
half of the Chalcedonian Definition which Barth interprets as
aimed at Monist excesses. But these diverse and indestructible
natures are not, as it were, hermetically sealed from each other
but participate in each other in a complete and indestructible
union. This is the point of the second half of the Chalcedonian
Definition which in Barth's view is directed against Dualist
excesses. The personal or hypostatic union must therefore be
balanced by the communication of the natures, their
participation with each other within the personal union.

This can be expressed in different ways. There is first the
sharing of the attributes (the classical *communicatio
idiomatum*). For Barth this is valid only from the divinity to
the humanity and not vice versa. Thus he accepts the title
'Mother of God (*Theotokos*) for the Blessed Virgin but not the
deification or divinisation of man. The humanity is that of God
but the divinity is not the divinity of man. There is also a
participation in grace, but this must not be carried to the point
of betraying the constancy of God or implying the deification
of man. The leading case here is the sinlessness or perfect
obedience of Christ. His sinlessness and impossibility of
sinning breaks our sinfulness and impossibility of not sinning.
He also participates in the Spirit beyond measure, but here
there is a qualitative as well as a quantitative difference from
themselves. Finally there is a third way of describing the
participation of the natures. The Incarnation is an event, an
actuality, an operation between God and man fulfilled in Jesus
Christ. It results in a history and is therefore objective but not
static. Thus Humiliation and Exaltation are not so much two

different and successive states, but two opposed but strictly related moments in that history which operate together and interpenetrate each other. In the Incarnation God becomes man, not that man might become God but that he might come to God. Its subject is Jesus Christ in his history, in this history, this operation, this event. Barth is clearly right that the personal or hypostatic union cannot be understood apart from an active relation between the two natures (*op. cit.*, IV, ii, pp. 1–154).

This is a massive piece of Christology constructed on classical lines and setting the concept of the *Enhypostasia* within a genuinely religious framework. Barth can employ the ontological framework of the classical Christology with considerable skill but he is much on his guard against too static an approach to the event of Jesus Christ or the tendency to regard Christology as a mere exercise in the manipulation of logical categories. The various stages in his argument are carefully checked by reference to his Person and Work as a whole and arise from the reality of Jesus Christ as fact and event. His Christology is certainly a serious candidate for truth.

Some criticisms may however be made. The premise of Revelation is the sheet anchor of his whole *Church Dogmatics*. Some may wonder whether the content or pack of Revelation is as extensive as he claims. How far 'Jesus Christ, Very God and Very man' is directly or explicitly contained in the New Testament may be disputed. It can certainly be regarded as a legitimate, even an inevitable, inference from the New Testament data as a whole rather than as a repetition in summary form of what is explicitly stated in the New Testament itself. The exegetical task precedes doctrinal construction and raises its own problems. Again is Barth always consistent with himself? In his theological exposition of John 1.14 he seems to exclude any relation of action and reaction between the Word and the flesh. The one is subject, the other predicate, the one is active, the other passive. How is this consistent with his final section on the communication of the natures? Can his claim that the incarnate Lord assumed an Adamic, sinful humanity be harmonised with his apparent claim that he enjoyed the impossibility of sinning? Possibly the absence of a single context to his discussion through the division of his treatment into four different sections handicaps him more than he imagines. His firm rejection of an impersonal manhood and his description of the human nature of the incarnate Lord as a man in full concrete actuality is much to be welcomed but although the main lines of his discussion are clear enough (apart from a distinction between personality and individuality) he never successfully clarifies the difference between Person or *hypostasis* in the classical sense and personality in modern psychological usage. Perhaps wisely he prefers to keep as close as possible to the traditional terminology but many will find a serious weakness here in his exposition.

Emil Brunner, a former colleague of Barth's and later his opponent, attempts to fill this gap (*The Mediator*; Lutterworth Press, 1967, pp. 345–54). He distinguishes between Person and personality. The former, a suprahistorical reality, is supplied by the Word; the latter, an observable historical reality, belongs to the human nature. He finds a possible parallel in the doctrine of the self. There is a distinction between the transcendental ego and the empirical self, or the self as knowing and experiencing and the self as known and experienced by others. In ourselves these are two aspects of one and the same self. In Christ the place of the transcendental ego is taken by the Word. If the distinction holds, Person and *hypostasis* are identical while personality is included in the nature. But, as we have seen, personality in its modern sense, while not identical with either *hypostasis* or nature, has points of contact with both. Dr Mascall, another leading champion of the classical solution, claims (*Christ, the Christian and the Church*; Longmans, 1946, pp. 38–41) that any attempt to establish a relation between person and personality confuses two different sets of ideas and is virtually a category mistake. Person is an ontological idea, personality belongs to the vocabulary of psychology. The two terminologies are not identical and it is idle to use one to fill out the other. The theologian should stick to his own set of terms which were deliberately intended to rescue Christology from the morass of ancient psychology.

The modern use of personality, consciousness and will presents similar dangers and the theologian must resist the temptation to be manoeuvred off his own ground. Admittedly there are grave difficulties in offering a psychology of Christ. The gospels display no interest in the consciousness of Christ and, as Mascall points out, we cannot tell by introspection what it meant to be the incarnate Lord. Many however will hold that if the theologian wishes to remain within earshot of his own contemporaries he cannot altogether ignore the possibilities of terms like personality, will and consciousness. Otherwise his preferred terms like person and nature will invite the application of Occam's razor and be liquidated accordingly. Problems of this type make it impossible to close our christological file at this point without considering what else can be said.

While the classical view affirms of God the Logos (following Cyril) that 'What he was, he remained; what he was not, he assumed', the Kenotic Movement, influential in the nineteenth and early twentieth centuries, modified the first part of this statement so far as the period of the Incarnation was concerned. The place of God, the Son of God, within the Holy Trinity was not affected, but for the purpose of the Incarnation he either laid aside or limited himself so as not to use some attributes of the Godhead such as omnipotence, omniscience and omnipresence which seemed irreconcilable with the existence of a complete humanity. Its biblical starting-point was the Kenosis passage in Phil. 2 which contains the vital word 'he emptied himself' (*ekenōsen*) but has no direct bearing on the problems which the movement tried to solve. As some exponents of Kenoticism saw, the christology of the fathers gave the new movement little support. Even Cyril's repeated use of the word is controlled by the christological principle noted above. His interpretation of *kenosis* as contraction, or reduction of compass (*meiosis*), should however be borne in mind. The negative adverb 'unchangeably' in the Chalcedonian Definition might even be deemed to exclude Kenoticism in advance. It was however originally aimed at the Arian doctrine of the incarnate Logos as a depotentiated God appearing in the flesh.

The movement originated on the Continent in the earlier part of the nineteenth century where it took two forms. More moderate Kenoticists spoke of the self-limitation of the Logos; a more radical view maintained his self-deprivation, the abandonment for a time of his self-consciousness as a divine subject. This suggestion of a kind of cosmic absenteeism or of an unlucid interval or thirty or more years in the eternal self-consciousness of the Logos is a gratuitous piece of mythology which raised the almost insoluble problem of the resumption of what had been lost.

British Kenoticism began later in the century and followed the more moderate line. The groundwork was supplied by the liberal Anglo-Catholic theologian (later Bishop successively of Worcester and Oxford) Charles Gore (1853–1932) in his Bampton Lectures for 1891 *The Incarnation of the Son of God* and the long second Dissertation of the companion volume.

Despite much criticism in his own day, Gore's treatment was immensely influential and he never seriously modified his views. The main problem for him was the tension between the omniscience of God and the human ignorance of Christ. Conservative Old Testament scholars frequently used a christological argument against the source-critical method in the Old Testament. Christ ascribed the Pentateuch to Moses and the Psalter to David, and that was the end of the matter. Gore was also concerned to justify a more realistic exegesis of the gospels against the tendency to psychological docetism arising from the heavy accentuation of the impassibility and immutability of the Logos even within the Incarnation to which the classical view was frequently exposed from Patristic times. For Gore the Incarnation involved a measure of *kenosis* (viewed from below) as well as of sacrifice (viewed from above). These two concepts are inseparably linked throughout his christology. He emphatically rejects theories of self-abandonment as a theological nonsense inconsistent with the divine self-sacrifice. The only possible alternative was the theory of a dual life-centre in the incarnate Lord. He who knows and does all things in the Father began to live under a new life-centre when he assumed manhood. Gore honestly admitted that the only difficulty of this view was how to conceive it. But the real problem of his christology lies elsewhere. He sometimes writes as if the incarnate Logos merely restrained his divine prerogatives; at other times he thinks more radically of surrender or abandonment. Nor is it clear whether this restraint or abandonment was a single act of will prior to the Incarnation or a continuing process within it. The religious nerve of his theory, the Incarnation as an act of divine self-sacrifice, is probably more acceptable than his detailed christological mapwork. In Gore's own theory *kenosis* ought to work better than it does.

A notable advance in British Kenotic theory was made by another Anglo-Catholic theologian, Frank Weston (1871–1924), later Bishop of Zanzibar. He had listened to Gore's Bampton Lectures as a student and his book *The One Christ* (Longmans, 1907) was a notable achievement. His Christology approximates to the classical solution but it is probably better regarded as a moderate form of Kenoticism. His coordinates, careful biblical exegesis and respect for the authority of the fathers, were identical with those of Gore. There is however no more talk about self-abandonment but only of self-restraint; and this he regards as the standing condition of the Incarnation and not merely as a prior act of will.

The Person who became incarnate is purely divine. The Incarnation cannot modify his true life in the eternal Godhead. The *Kenosis* involved in the Incarnation was no abandonment of the divine atttributes either in whole or part but a self-limitation or law of restraint which extended continuously over the whole field of his incarnate being. It even applied to his relation to the Father. As incarnate the Son can pray to the Father. This restraint is involved in the doctrine that the Logos assumed to himself a complete ensouled human nature. The subject of the manhood is the Logos himself, but the self-limiting Logos. The human nature is neither a mere conditioning nor a theoretically detachable man. Apart from the qualification 'the self-limiting Logos' Karl Barth would agree.

The Incarnation is therefore both a revelation of God and a disclosure of man. It is the former because the Logos is its true and proper subject. It is the latter because perfect manhood is not autonomous or independent manhood but a God-aided and God-directed humanity. The law of restraint is not simply a prior act of will leading to an alteration in the nature of the Logos through the abandonment of attributes. Rather it lies within the fact of being incarnate and extends over the whole area of the incarnate life. Its measure is the capacity of manhood at its best to contain and to mediate the life of the Logos. This recalls the insight of Irenaeus in the second century: 'He filled the manhood with as much of the Godhead as it was able to bear.'

But this process of self-restraint on the part of the Logos through the assumed manhood was also progressive. As the humanity developed, so its capacity to reflect and mediate the Logos increased. This cannot be interpreted in terms of loss or self-abandonment but as a voluntary restriction of the Logos to what can be mediated through the humanity at any given time. Weston illustrates his point by models drawn from human life, the surrender or sacrifice of a greater vocation for a lesser for the sake of love; though he is careful not to claim too much for them.

The self-limiting Logos, then, never touches life at any point except through the medium of his humanity. Without alteration or subtraction he is from eternity to eternity one person of the Holy Trinity. This set of relations subsists and continues even within the Incarnation. But in Time he becomes incarnate, adding to himself a complete ensouled human nature with a new set of relations. The measures of this humanity he permits to prevail over himself and thus manifests himself not as the unqualified and unconditioned Logos but as the self-limiting Logos. Within the incarnate Lord there are two entities: the Logos and his humanity; the one personal, the other not independently represented. We cannot speak of a double life-centre, for there is a single way of going about things whereby the Logos is always both restricted and mediated by his own humanity. In the Incarnation there is a single subject, a single self-consciousness, the self-limiting Logos acting in and through his humanity. But there are two sets of relations reciprocating and not merely alternating within the incarnate life.

This is a careful and reverent theory. Against Cyril (whom he often resembles) he uses the human soul of Christ to better advantage in his christology and deals more realistically with the measures of the humanity. Against the more radical Kenoticists he will have nothing to do with theories of self-abandonment. He writes consistently of self-restraint, which he regards as a principle continuously at work throughout the whole Incarnation and not simply as a prior act of will on the part of the Logos. He seems to operate with two frameworks for the selfhood of Christ, one person, two natures' and one self-consciousness, two sets of relations, without considering whether these are identical or not. That Weston's exegesis, like Gore's, is rather dated is perhaps unfair comment.

P. T. Forsyth (1848–1921) in his book *The Person and Place of Jesus Christ* (Independent Press, 1909) reached very similar conclusions to those of Weston. An orthodox Congregationalist, he took as his second control (besides Scripture) not the fathers, but the criterion of religious experience. His style is highly individual and somewhat difficult, but thoroughly to master his book is still an enriching intellectual exercise.

He argues that for those who accept a pre-existence Christology only two options are open: an accommodation Christology or some form of *Kenosis*. Christian Redemption requires divine descent into human life. Its subject and therefore its mode was unique. He has a sharp eye for the paradoxes of the Incarnation. The Son is from eternity to eternity and yet experiences growth in time. God cannot be tempted, yet the incarnate Lord experiences temptations. God is omniscient, yet Christ not only professes ignorance on some points but also seems limited to the knowledge available in his own day. To describe the process of *kenosis* which is involved here, Forsyth writes of retraction rather than of abandonment or restraint. I am afraid that I cannot find a better analogy than the retractable undercariage of an aircraft. It is there the whole time for use at take-off and landing but withdrawn not only from view but also from active participation in the flight of the aircraft. This model is far from ideal. It is mechanical and subpersonal and cannot adequately reflect the uniqueness of the mode of the Incarnation. On this view the divine attributes are still there. They are neither jettisoned nor abandoned, but withdrawn not simply from view but also from circulation or active use. The idea of withdrawal from actuality to potentiality is difficult because for us an attribute is always actual. It is something which can be grasped intellectually by means of which an object or a person can be identified or experienced. Like Weston, Forsyth offers some human parallels such as a man who gives up a career of academic brilliance for family reasons. Usually they cover either the surrender of one actuality for another or of a potentiality for a different actuality. The point lies in the motive; a sacrifice made for the sake of love.

Forsyth's reminder that the mode of the Incarnation cannot be adequately paralleled because the fact itself is unique must always be kept in mind. On the temptations of Christ, Forsyth makes the interesting suggestion that, while Christ as the incarnate Son may have enjoyed the blessed impossibility of sinning, he could not know this under the conditions of the Incarnation and therefore faced them as if the possibility of not sinning alone was his. This ingenious proposal may be too slick to be completely convincing.

Forsyth's second contribution to Christology develops a theme already present in Weston. Corresponding to the *kenosis* of the Godhead there is a *plerosis* or fulfilment of the manhood. The diminuendo of the Godhead is matched by a crescendo of the manhood. What the Logos retracted as God when he became incarnate, this he progressively regained as man. This represents an attempt to combine within the limits of a single theory the two rhythms of descent and ascent which have often been regarded either as successive states or regarded as alternatives and developed into divisive systems. But is this a genuine reconciliation of the two approaches or a loose combination of some elements of one system with some insights of the other? Or are they complementary truths which cannot be brought successfully within the limits of a single theory? Forsyth is sometimes inclined to speak of rhythms or movements without asking the further question 'Who or what moves?' At such times he tends to become obscure. Yet his theory is a fruitful example of the Kenotic approach.

At first sight the differences between the classical solution and moderate Kenotic Christology seem relatively small. The divine Logos remains within the Holy Trinity even though for Kenoticism the subject of the incarnate life is the self-limiting Logos. No less than the classical Christology, Kenoticism represents a christology from the side of God. Both views accept and seek to provide for 'the measures of the humanity', though Kenotic views go considerably further than the classical Christology in their assessment of the place of the humanity. A main difference between the two schools of thought is that, while the classical view accepts the full co-presence of the two natures, divine and human, and recognises some interaction between them, at least in the direction of the divine towards the human, Kenotic theologians see the divinity as 'encapsulated' within the humanity, both limited by it and mediated through it. For Weston during the incarnate life even the Son's relation to the Father is contained within the limits set by his manhood. This lends point to Mascall's formidable objection that Kenoticism is virtually Monophysitism in reverse. Monophysitism evacuates or truncates the manhood in the supposed best interests of the divinity. Kenoticism moves in the opposite direction.

A partial justification of the Kenotic approach to Christology can be found not only in the psychological docetism of much of the exegesis of exponents of the classical Christology but also in the frontier questions which they find it necessary to discuss. Thus Aquinas admits the possibility of a kind of communicated omnipotence and omniscience in the incarnate life of our Lord though he moves with great caution and a multitude of distinctions. Mascall finds it difficult to determine whether the most notable miracles of Our Lord are to be regarded as acts of pure omnipotence or available to a perfect humanity assumed by God the Logos. In common with all sensible christologians he dismisses the possibility that 'in the plain and obvious sense of the words, the human mind of the Babe of Bethlehem was thinking, as he lay in the manger, of the Procession of the Holy Ghost, the theorems of hydrodynamics, the novels of Jane Austen and the Battle of

Hastings' (*Christ, the Christian and the Church*; Longmans, 1946, p.53). Yet the furthest that he is prepared to go is the admission that the human knowledge of our Lord was not inconsistent with genuine growth and development. For a Kenoticist questions about omnipotence and omniscience are too remote to seem relevant to Christology. We may recall the distinction (common to the period) between the metaphysical attributes which supply the conceptual groundwork of the classical doctrine of God and his moral attributes, which fill in the even more significant portrayal of his character. Barth's claim that the condescension of God is an act of his free omnipotence is a daring attempt to fill in the gap between the two. Yet on his part the Kenoticist must be able to offer a reasonable account of the miracles of Jesus and what we have ventured to call the divine hinterland to the Person of Christ in his life, ministry and teaching. Barth's distinction between God giving himself and God giving himself away is relevant here, though it may not be easy to draw with precision.

A further difference between the two main christologies from the side of God concerns their selection of categories. The classical solution employed ontological categories like person and nature, and during its long development developed considerable skill in their deployment. The Kenoticists turned to the current vocabulary of personality, consciousness and will and the idea of a self as composed of its relations. Clearly the ontological and the psychological vocabularies do not pair off easily with each other. They arise from different backgrounds and are even designed to answer different questions. But neither can be accused of treachery to the gospel. Both are exercises in the translation of the New Testament data. The Kenoticists can as little be blamed for using the thought-forms available to them as the fathers for employing the notions of contemporary metaphysics. The only question is which idiom is better adapted to express what needs to be said in christology. Indeed christology may be the kind of field in which both explorations are admissible, ontology because of the divine involvement in the Incarnation, psychology because it is in and through manhood that this involvement takes place.

Kenoticists of the moderate type made much use of limitation and restraint as a major clue. Here they were certainly not in error. Indeed it was suggested that kenotic language can be appropriately used in the doctrine of Creation. The will of God, absolute in itself, regroups itself to allow the reality of secondary causes within the created order, even to the point of allowing them a considerable role in their own evolution. If one object of creation is to promote the free obedience of sons with the alternative possibility of the resistance movement of rebels, then it cannot be regarded as a piece of divine puppetry in which God pulls all the strings. It can reasonably be argued that the will of God has different ways of going about things at the various levels of evolution. In creation the will of God seems limited and expressed in ways which correspond to the nature of the subject-matter to which it applies itself. If this is the case, there is a parallel between the action of God in Creation and Incarnation, though since immanence and Incarnation are not one thing but two, the analogy is not exact. It may nevertheless be a point of fruitful exploration in both fields. Without denying the priority of the divine action in both doctrines, an approach to the doctrine of Creation through secondary causes and to the doctrine of the Incarnation through the concept of *kenosis* at least deserves careful consideration. The distinction drawn by Bishop Gore, that the doctrine of the Incarnation involves divine sacrifice viewed from above and *kenosis* viewed from below, deserves more attention than it seems to have received. *Kenosis* can be regarded as a kind of worm's-eye view of the divine condescension.

Exponents of the classical solution find Kenoticism vulnerable at a further point which for them is fatal to its success. The notion of a depotentiated God, stripping himself of attributes, retracting them not only from view but also from circulation (Forsyth) or even God limiting himself, seems to them not only a highly mythological conception but also renders him valueless for the purposes of Revelation and Redemption. Against Arianism or any crude notion of alteration or change in the Godhead arising from the Incarnation it is already excluded by the negative adverb 'unchangeably' in the Chalcedonian Definition. It has its full force against theories of abandonment or loss of attributes, but it cannot hold against a doctrine of self-limitation or self-restraint. On the assumption of the logical incompatibility of the infinite and the finite the Kenoticist argues that for sheer love's sake (Gore's note of sacrifice) the Logos loved not his metaphysical fullness of being to the uttermost but emptied himself in order to make possible the encapsulation of the Godhead within a human life. The vital difference here is the concept of the self-limiting Logos and it might be thought that this was the precondition of (or at least all of one piece with) the Cross. Mascall in his criticism of Kenoticism avoids the description of the humanity as a limitation. He prefers the neutral word 'instrument', presumably as the perfectly calibrated, rationally ensouled medium of the divine self-expression in deed and word. But surely it is both, and the one because it is also the other. It is a limitation making the Logos 'bearable' (to use Cyril's word) to man, and the expression of God's revealing and redeeming purpose for finite and fallen man. The insight of Irenaeus: 'He filled the manhood with as much of the Godhead as it was able to bear', unites both the positive and negative aspects of the humanity of the incarnate Lord.

A different set of objections from the moderate Dualist standpoint is raised by Donald Baillie (formerly Professor of Divinity at St Andrews and a distinguished theologian of the Church of Scotland) in his book *God was in Christ* (Faber, 1948, pp. 94–8). He defines the view which he is criticising as follows: 'The Son of God, the Second Person of the Trinity, the Divine Logos, laid aside his divine attributes (omnipotence, omniscience and omnipresence) and lived for a period on earth within the limits of the humanity' (pp. 94–5). He admits frankly the attractions of this view. It apparently enables us to combine a full faith in the deity of Christ with a completely frank treatment of his life on earth as the life of a man, 'It gets away entirely from the docetism which has so often infected Christology. It is able to go the whole way in using human categories about Jesus; he lived a man's life, his mind worked as a man's mind, his knowledge was limited to human knowledge, his equipment to human equipment' (p. 95). Although he was 'personally identical with the eternal Son of God one in essence with the Father, and equal in power and glory'. He 'emptied himself' in becoming incarnate of those attributes ... which differentiate God from man, so that the life which He lived on earth was a truly human life subject to the conditions and limitations of humanity' (p. 95). This is an excellent statement of the Kenotic position but Baillie finds it exposed to formidable objections.

The first is derived from a question of Archbishop William Temple in his book *Christus Veritas* (Macmillan, 1924, pp. 142–3). 'What was happening to the rest of the universe during the period of our Lord's earthly life? ... To say that ... the Creative Word was so self-emptied as to have no being except in the Infant Jesus, is to assert that for a certain period the history of the world was let loose from the control of the Creative Word.' This objection would be fatal to any theory of self-abandonment; it lacks force against a doctrine of self-limitation which relates only to the Incarnation. The ultimate subject of the incarnate life is not the limited but the self-limiting Logos, and the recognition that there are self-limitations or retractions of the specifically divine attributes for the purpose of the Incarnation and within the incarnate life does not necessarily involve the consequences in the universe which Temple fears.

Baillie's second objection runs as follows: if Kenoticism is true, whether in its more extreme or even in its moderate form, it offers 'a story of a temporary manifestation of God (a theophany) in which He who formerly was God changed Himself temporarily into man, or exchanged His divinity for humanity'. Even though he remains the ultimate subject of the Incarnation, and therefore retains his personal identity, 'He has divested Himself of the *distinctively divine* attributes; which would imply, if language means anything, that in becoming human He ceased to be divine' (p. 96).

This argument is relevant against a radical theory of Kenosis which could well be interpreted as meaning that he was God first, then man, then God again. But asking a Temple-like question of moderate Kenoticism, 'What is left of the

Logos within the Incarnation', would invite the Pauline rejoinder 'Much every way'. The Logos remains the ultimate centre of the incarnate life. The still centre of divine saving love is unimpaired even though it is channelled into the encompassing humanity which he assumes. The reminder of Weston and Forsyth, that what was restrained or limited was progressively displayed through the humanity as it became capable of bearing it, must also be borne in mind. All that was limited or restrained was what in the nature of Godhead was neither 'veiled in flesh' (Apollinarianism) nor changed into humanity (Pagan notions of metamorphosis); but limited by the very act of the Logos himself to what perfect manhood can mediate to men.

Other critics had made the point that, if the divesting of the divine attributes was difficult to envisage, their resumption after the Incarnation raised an equally serious problem. Baillie is too wise to take over this criticism as it stands. His point is different and is directed against both extreme and moderate Kenoticists. He asks 'Was the *kenosis* merely temporary, confined to the period of the Incarnation?' and assumes that the answer must be 'Yes'. There is a sense in which the Incarnation is temporary', since there is a finality, speciality and decisiveness about it which we neglect at our peril. Baillie is concerned here with the permanence of our Lord's humanity after the Ascension. He writes:

> The presupposition of the [*sc.* Kenotic] theory is that the distinctive divine attributes [of omniscience etc.] and the distinctive human attributes [of finitude] cannot be united simultaneously in one life: that is why the Incarnation is explained as a *kenosis*. Therefore when the days of His flesh come to an end, Christ resumes His divine attributes, and His *kenosis*, his humanity, comes to an end' (p. 97).

The shorthand expression 'his *kenosis*, his humanity' needs unpacking before its meaning becomes clear. As Kenoticists use the term, *kenosis* is an attempt to clarify the conditions of the Incarnation as viewed from below. The humanity is both the limiting condition into which the Logos descends and the vehicle of his revealing and redemptive purpose. Christian theology has always spoken of the glorified humanity which, after the Ascension, Christ brought back with him into the eternal realm. Where the objection goes wrong is in its opening words. The incompatibility between the distinctive divine attributes and the finitude of human nature applies, and can only apply, to the finite conditions under which the Incarnation took place. Once the specific conditions of the Incarnation were completed, there seems no greater difficulty about the glorification of the humanity than in the resumption of the divine attributes which were limited or restrained freely by the eternal Son of God at his entry into the conditions of the Incarnation.

A Christology from the side of God, whether in its strict classical form or in the shape of a moderate Kenoticism, is therefore still a perfectly viable type of Christology. It gets the direction of the Incarnation right as an act of the divine initiative. It provides for the divine involvement in the incarnate life, though more richly and obviously on the classical view than in the Kenotic theories. On the other hand Kenoticism appears to have the edge in the place which it assigns to the humanity. The problem of the classical view is to clarify the concept of the *Enhypostasia* and to re-state it in more contemporary terms. The crux for Kenoticism is to explain on its own premises the extent and nature of the self-limitation of the Son of God implied in his Incarnation. The ontological categories employed by the classical view are more stable and clear-cut than the psychological terminology used by the Kenoticists; though as a legitimate exercise in thought translation the latter cannot be excluded. With some hesitation I opt for a moderate Kenoticism of the type expounded by Weston and Forsyth.

We must however examine other alternatives in Christology and attempt to assess their adequacy as explorations of the doctrine.

5   Christologies from the side of Man

CHRISTIAN theology has often proceeded by a series of oscillations in which what has been neglected or undervalued in one period has become the corner-stone of the next. This does not reflect an intention to 'walk unruly'; still less does it cast doubt either on the reality of its subject-matter or the ability and integrity of the theologian. It arises rather from the 'many-sided wisdom of God' which resists all attempts to domesticate and control it. There are however fashions in theology which pass and change as they are corrected by new insights and fresh emphases. Thus in the doctrine of God the stress on divine immanence of the older Liberalism was corrected by the emphasis upon the transcendence of God in the thought of Karl Barth and his followers, and this again has been followed by a fresh accentuation of immanence in the last twenty years.

But there is another and yet more important fact about theology. It needs an effective 'sparring partner' in secular thought. At first this was found in philosophy; whether Platonism, sometimes called the 'perennial philosophy', or Aristotelianism, as in the great synthesis of Thomas Aquinas. But great changes have taken place in the philosophical scene which have made the prospect of an alliance unwelcome to philosophy and unpromising for theology. More recently attempts have been made to strike up a working partnership with history. By its very nature Christianity has an important stake in history. Phrases like historical revelation, the historic faith, the Jesus of history, indicate as much. But the failure of the old quest for the historical Jesus and its aftermath has shown the limitations of this projected 'Grand Alliance'.

The categories of psychology have been explored in

86

Christology with differing intentions and with unequal success. While science is professionally neutral in matters of theology, it is natural that the theologian should listen carefully to what science is saying to the Churches and try to construct an answering theology. This is inevitable, and perhaps not even regrettable, provided that at the end of the day one gospel is not substituted for another.

Attempts to construct a Christology from the side of man represent an oscillation in the study of the subject. Such attempts seek to take account of the shift in emphasis which has taken place since the construction of the classical solution and, even more important, to construct an answering Christology fitted to the needs of modern man. Bonhoeffer asked 'Who is Jesus Christ for us to-day?' and others will be haunted by the same question.

 Bishop John Robinson (*The Human Face of God*; SCM Press, 1973, pp. 19–32) notes four main changes of emphasis which in his view demand a fresh starting-point in Christology from a new angle. The first is the new approach to myth in the Bible. Until relatively recently myth was taken quite realistically as providing the framework for all life. Now it is equated with the fictional or the unreal. Robinson's attitude to myth will be familiar to all readers of *Honest to God*; he rejects the Up and Down myth, 'the God in the gaps' and the supranaturalist frame as a whole. Myth can however be interpreted as a form of theological italics, a way of indicating the special importance of events or situations. It is one kind of language, one 'story' to be told alongside a different and more readily acceptable account of the same phenomena. Thus in the section of the Apostles' Creed dealing with the Son, the clause 'suffered under Pontius Pilate' (an event in history) is combined with 'Sitteth at the right hand of the Father', which cannot be understood with the same uncompromising literalness. For some modern men this raises a serious problem; the precise diagnosis and interpretation of myth. Is it simply a method of expressing the supranaturalist frame which could be retained without its aid; or must its rejection or restatement bring down the framework as a whole? Some articles in the Creed are obviously couched in mythical or pictorial language, but is the quality of the Virgin Birth, the Ascension and the Second Coming as events necessarily destroyed by the mythical language in which they are, and perhaps must be, conveyed? Can their doctrinal significance be retained if their status as events in the past or the future is abandoned? There is a danger here of 'throwing out the baby with the bathwater'. For Robinson the supranaturalist frame is dead beyond recall. The trouble is that for many of us it won't lie down as readily as he would wish.

The second shift concerns the status of metaphysical questions. 'What myth is to the imagination metaphysics is to the intellect. It is the way of trying to state what is most real, most true, ultimate' (*The Human Face of God*, pp. 22–3). Robinson himself admits that we cannot dispense with metaphysics altogether but restricts its range to a reality which is otherwise evidenced for us. In philosophy metaphysics has come under serious challenge from empiricism, logical positivism and linguistic analysis. How far these represent a shift in the basic questions themselves or simply in the conceptual tools used to discuss them is a debatable point. What Robinson is really excluding is the use of metaphysics as a point of entry into a 'superworld of divine objects'. This merely repeats his distrust of the supranaturalist frame which we have already noted in discussion of myth. But the downfall, real or alleged, of the older metaphysics is not an additional reason for Robinson's earlier rejection; for metaphysics initiates nothing, but merely organises whatever is believed to exist into a coherent and systematic framework. The extent to which Robinson is prepared to go is indicated by his hesitations about the traditional interpretation of the pre-existence of Christ, his uncreated reality as the Second Person of the Trinity and his Eternal Generation by the Father. This cannot fairly be debited to metaphysics and is in any case a high price to pay for an 'answering Christology'. His second objection to the older metaphysical theology lies in the charge that the vocabulary of substance is unduly static. Once again the charge is not fully justified. While the use of substance and person formed part of the attempt to provide a more stable and coherent framework for Christian theology, there is abundant evidence that the older metaphysical theology made a serious, and not unsuccessful, attempt to handle dynamic realities. The older framework may be neither as defective or disposable as he appears to think.

The third main shift of emphasis is described in a phrase taken from van Buren: 'the dissolution of the absolute'. This describes the loss of appetite for far-reaching philosophical systems which seek to give explanations of the universe as a whole. Its opposite is pluralism or relativism; the recognition of many truths relative to each other and none making an absolute claim to account for everything. It would be a gross misunderstanding to equate this with scepticism. This is certainly not the case with Robinson and other advocates of this view. He argues strongly that there are three different approaches to Christology: the mythical, the ontological and the functional, of which he greatly prefers the third. Those who find his preference inadequate to the facts have an equal right to opt for one of the other two, provided that they listen carefully to his arguments. Integrity and charity must not be set at loggerheads; they are two sides of the same coin. Robinson notes that this shift of emphasis must affect the claims made for the finality of Christ, or at least the way in which this is expressed. To say merely that Christ is a clue, or even the clue for me, would be untrue to the Church's witness to Christ. Robinson concludes that he is 'the man for others', or even the 'man for all'. He is 'the human face of God' or a 'window into God at work'. This is no negligible claim. From a different viewpoint I should want to say that he is God's clue for all men, as solid on the divine side with God as on the human side with ourselves. The difference here is vital and should not be underestimated even in the interests of an answering Christology.

The fourth point in Robinson's analysis is the question of historicity where the risks, so far as the gospels are concerned, has become higher during the present century. We are in full agreement in protesting against some of the absurdities which pass for assured critical conclusions. Robinson makes a skilful and, on the whole, a conservative use of the criterion of 'the credibility gap' between the facts and their interpretation which must not become too large if their interpretation is to be sustained. Three possibilities are open with regard to the gospels: complete historical certainty, immunity from historical research and historical risk. We should both accept the third, but I should want to add that a fair degree of probability exists at most points in the gospel tradition which materially affect Christology. We are not very far apart here.

These four changes in perspective lead Robinson, in the interests of an answering Christology, to approach the doctrine from a fresh and radically different starting-point. Three ways of approach are admissible: the mythological, which uses the picture language of late Judaism and early Christianity; the ontological, which translates the same truths from poetic to philosophical categories; or the functional which 'looks as if it is saying much less than the other two, having neither the robust rotundity of personification (of the first), nor the solidity of substance (of the second). Yet it is another, equally serious way of asserting identity—but in terms of verbs rather than substantives or substances' (*The human Face of God*, p. 183). Elsewhere (p. 194) he speaks of 'the high language of verbs in which the New Testament speaks'. The accent will therefore fall on the nature of what is done rather than upon the Person of the doer; or, more simply, on what Christ does, not on what he is. In Robinson's view it is possible to start from Jesus as a man and yet to satisfy the requirement to say divine things about him without removing him from his human context. A functional or moral unity between the Father and the Son will provide all that Christology requires without the need to employ metaphysical categories or to invoke the supra-naturalist frame.

Robinson's argument is cumulative. It begins from below and works upwards by successive stages. Jesus is a man, a complete and particular human being. This is where the disciples themselves began and the early sermons in Acts are faithful to this insight. The classical statement strongly insisted that he was perfect in manhood or perfect man, but its further claim that he was also perfect in Godhead or perfect God set up a continual tendency to psychological docetism, a flinching away from his more poignantly human experiences or their reduction to a scale more appropriate to the incarnate Logos. For Robinson the acceptance of a human soul and will in Christ is not enough, since it ignores the nexus of biological, historical and social relationships which for us make up a human being. Older theologians had found it hard enough to handle environmental influences on Jesus. The role of heredity is even more difficult for the classical view. The decoding of genes presents a more serious threat to traditional Christology than the recognition of the first-century Jewish conditioning of his human mind. A genuine humanity, as distinct from a divine visitor from outside, must be a true product of the human process with all the prehistory of the race in his genes.

Robinson now proceeds to test for reaction. On the basis of the inclusion of women in the Matthean genealogy, all of doubtful antecedents or lineage, he is prepared to consider the possibility that Jesus was born out of wedlock. He is not saying that he accepts this view, but merely claims that, on his premises, it cannot be dismissed on the grounds of inappropriateness or impropriety. The charge is certainly raised in the Jewish Talmud but the explanation that this is simply a hostile inversion of the Virgin Birth tradition is a good deal more probable. With a similar motive Robinson raises a number of questions about the sexuality of Jesus and insists that we must be free to ask them; though he admits frankly that the gospels provide no material for an answer. That he should be free to ask them is one thing; whether in the complete absence of evidence they are sensible questions is quite another. Certainly the human nature of Christ must have included sexuality. In the light of his mission and vocation it cannot have played a significant role in his life.

Robinson now passes to Jesus as 'the Man', the second Adam or, as Luther described him 'the proper man'. Clearly this cannot mean 'the man who had everything' or 'the man with the mostest'. This is not the Jesus of the gospel tradition. He is the Man, as Robinson finely says, in his 'radical integrity, obedience, courage, freedom and inner victory' (p. 77). His sinlessness was not an itemised steering-clear of sin but a positive life of obedience. 'He learned obedience in the school of suffering' (Heb. 5.8). It admitted of growth and was

attended by moral struggles and conflict. Gethsemane and the
Temptation narratives of the gospels are relevant here. He was
'tempted at all points like ourselves, yet without sin' (Heb.
4.13). While it is true that the full force of temptation is felt by
the greatest saint rather than the hardened sinner, Robinson
claims that there must be some point of reference within the
one who is tempted. A life of perfect obedience is one thing; an
in-built inability to do anything else quite another. Robinson
clearly opts for the possibility of not sinning rather than the
impossibility of sinning. It is sometimes forgotten that this is a
matter which the Chalcedonian Definition leaves completely
open. This chapter shows Robinson at his most positive.

He next turns to Jesus as the Man of God. He admits that
the pressure to say divine things about Jesus in some form is
inseparable from the claim that he is the Christ. The mystery
of Christ is that he is the clue both to the meaning of history
and to the meaning of God at work. He speaks truly both
about God and about man. However we interpret it, he is, in
the classical formula, both truly God and truly man. He is the
true Logos of God if by that is meant the self-expressive
activity of God. For Robinson nothing must get in the way of
the divine initiative in Jesus but equally nothing must interfere
with his humanity; full, genuine and particular. The watershed
between Jesus as the Man and the Man about whom divine
things must be said is the Resurrection. The transition from
'Man of God' to 'God's Man' is made in the next chapter
which is devoted to the rest of the New Testament. Jesus is
God's Man as the divinely commissioned man, 'The man of
God's own choosing'. We must not return again to the subject
of the second chapter of this book except to note Robinson's
strong tendency to under-expound the content of passages like
Col. 1.15–20, and Heb. 1.1–3 and his comparative neglect of
the Johannine Prologue. References to the 'cosmic Christ' or
Christ as central to Creation are left in the air and the 'image
language' of the New Testament interpreted exclusively in
terms of the image of God in Gen. 1.26. Here the starting-point
of the concept may not be a completely adequate clue to its
New Testament application.

The crucial chapter for Robinson's whole enterprise is

entitled 'God for us'. Here, if anywhere, we must find the high
Christology which he has promised us, and his intention,
though not his performance, is not for a moment in doubt.
Jesus who was:

> one who was totally and utterly a man—and had never been
> anything other than a man, or more than a man—so
> completely embodied what was from the beginning the
> meaning and purpose of God's self-expression (whether
> conceived in terms of his Spirit, his Wisdom, his Word, or
> the intimately personal relationship of Sonship) that it could
> be said, and had to be said, of that man 'He was God's man'
> or 'God was in Christ', or even that he was 'God for us' (p.
> 179).

But how can Christ be God for us without ceasing to be truly a
man? His text is 'God was in Christ' (2 Cor. 5.19) and the
question which it suggests to him 'Does what we see in Jesus
actually bring us into contact with God at work, so that to
have seen him, met and be judged by him is to have seen, met
and been judged by God?' (p. 181) must be answered in the
affirmative. The Incarnation discloses the initiative and
involvement of God to a unique degree, as well as the human
response to it. Anything less would fall short of what the
Incarnation means.

Robinson illustrates his argument from the Father-Son
correlation of the Fourth Gospel. He claims that it can be
understood functionally without any ontological overtones. It
is the 'high language of verbs' to which he has already called
our attention. What the Father does, the Son does. Christ is the
very exegesis of God (John 1.18) and indeed is himself God
because as a man he is utterly transparent to another who is
greater than he (John 14.28) and indeed than all (John 10.29).
A moral unity, a functional Christology, might satisfy our
exegetical needs. But this is a strange and unacceptable
interpretation and many will find the traditional exegesis a
more reliable guide.

Jesus then is the one who dared to stand in the place of God
as his representative. His vocation is not to usurp or to replace
God but to represent him, the fearful calling to 'play God' (in a

sense very different from what we usually understand by the phrase), to be like God, to be God for men. He is the man who lived God. Much here may be possible mysticism, but the language and even the concepts are unbiblical. 'God for us' in this sense has no biblical parallel. Emmanuel or 'God with us' has a richer content and a deeper meaning. To speak of a man as 'living God' contradicts important biblical and theological insights into the relation between God and man. Within the limits which Robinson sets himself these are indeed high claims for Christ. The setting is functional but it may be described as 'high' functional. But will it work, and can we stop there? Robinson's coordinates are clear enough. His starting-point is the complete humanity of Jesus. The supranaturalist frame must be abandoned. The divine initiative and divine involvement must be retained at least at the functional level and expressed in terms of moral unity and spiritual identity.

What divides us here is not the importance of the moral unity of the Father and the Son in the operations of the Incarnation but its adequacy as the stopping place for christological inquiry. It may seem superficial criticism that verbs require substantives which can serve as subjects, and objects and which require in their turn to be placed in their appropriate logical contexts. In a footnote (p. 194) Robinson quotes the observation of the early German Reformer, Melanchthon 'To know Christ is to know his benefits, not, as the schoolmen teach, to contemplate his natures and the modes of his incarnation' (*Loci Communes*, Preface), but there is an important Scholastic principle that 'operation follows being' (*operari sequitur esse*). This calls attention to the need to offer an adequate ontological grounding for unity in activity or operation. The functional cannot replace the ontological as the final target for Christology. Penultimate answers cannot be substituted for the ultimate questions which insist on raising their heads. Despite his obvious intention to the contrary Robinson appears to be working a dimension short through his rejection of the supranaturalist frame and his refusal to push beyond the functional to the ontological in Christology.

We must first notice the substantial changes in theology as a whole which this reconstruction in Christology involves. Robinson's concern for a related theology leads him away from the transcendence of God in the direction of his immanence or from God in his 'In himselfhood' (*aseitas*) as the Scholastics put it, to his existence in relation to the universe. Here he is much indebted to Pittenger whose views will concern us later in this chapter. Robinson never tells us what place he assigns to the divine transcendence but his rejection of the supranaturalist frame and of metaphysics as a point of entry into a world of 'superobjects' warns us not to expect too much. The doctrine of the Trinity is also subjected to strain. The transition from Jesus the Son of God to God the Son in his full individuality is dismissed as a false trail. The Spirit, the Wisdom and the Word are only personifications which point to the self-expressive activity of God. A functional rather than an essential Trinity would probably serve his needs. He is so afraid of 'the God in the gaps' that he seems to pass over too easily the gaps between the Creator and the creature (as in the phrase 'the man who lived God') and between the Saviour and the sinner. The concept of the Incarnation as a divine rescue operation mounted at uttermost cost does not even receive the briefest and most dismissive mention. The first criticism of Robinson must therefore be that he is trying to produce a Christology which is a dimension short. The wonder is not that it seems inadequate but that it works as well as it does.

The divine initiative must be preserved at all costs. For Robinson this means that Jesus is the predestinate man, the man of God's own choosing; God's Man who stands in a close but a functional relation to God. Both the mythological and ontological approaches however speak of a divine descent; a downthrust into humanity which implies a richer initiative and, many would say, an indispensable aspect of the Incarnation. There is also a divine condescension to which the language of *kenosis* points. While his dismissal of Kenotic christologies is not as abrupt as some of its critics, he identifies the divine condescension (*kenosis*) with the fulfilment (*plerosis*) of the manhood. Weston and Forsyth had a truer instinct in their view that they were related but not identical aspects of a single process.

The divine involvement in the Incarnation is not negligible in Robinson's Christology; 'God was in Christ'. But his starting-point from the side of man and his functional approach make it difficult for him to give it full weighting. The classical statement made much of the double solidarity of the incarnate Lord with the Father and with ourselves. Robinson provides as full a solidarity with ourselves as anyone could wish. His attitude to the solidarity with God is more equivocal. Jesus can be called God because he is the man who lived God, who as man was utterly transparent to God. He is the human face of God or a window into God at work. At every point a human qualifier is introduced. He once notes the objection that the two solidarities are not being given equal weight but brushes it aside. He is ready enough to accuse the classical statement of weakening the humanity intolerably but he fails to see that he is exposed to the opposite danger. God was in Christ, the Word made flesh is one thing, a man utterly transparent to God, a man who lived God quite another. Robinson tries to bridge the gap in terms of love (*agapē*) but it is difficult to see how he can establish the difference between an identical and a similar love. Robinson asserts the former. Jesus presents but does not replace the love of God. He identifies himself with it through his utter transparency to God. But the prevenience of the love of God requires not an identification of Jesus with it, but God's self-identification of himself with man through Christ. Without this missing premise it is difficult to see that Robinson can provide what he means to convey. Only if God is more fully, more ontologically, involved in the Incarnation, can Robinson's explorations of the divinity of Christ follow as corollaries.

Much of his difficulty arises from his whole-hearted but somewhat uncritical acceptance of John Knox's dilemma, 'We can have the humanity without the pre-existence and we can have the pre-existence without the humanity. There is absolutely no way of having both.' (*The Humanity and Divinity of Christ*; Cambridge, 1967, p. 106). In order to adjust to his estimate of what is implied in solidarity with ourselves, he reduces considerably the corresponding solidarity with God, and thereby weakens the measure of divine involvement in the Incarnation. Despite its difficulties the classical doctrine of the two natures does the job of constructing a Christology considerably better than Robinson's view.

Similar conclusions are reached by an American Episcopalian scholar Norman Pittenger in his two books *The Word Incarnate* (Nisbet, 1959) and *Christology Reconsidered* (SCM Press, 1970). While Robinson, who freely acknowledges his debt to Pittenger, is primarily a New Testament scholar, Pittenger is first and foremost a systematic theologian. His treatment is more tightly constructed and less diffuse than that of Robinson, but they agree on the essential lines of their restatement of Christology and their rejection of the classical view, especially any doctrine of an impersonal humanity.

His philosophical background is derived from the Process philosophy of the Anglo-American mathematician and philosopher A. N. Whitehead (1861–1947) and a contemporary American philosopher Charles Hartshorne. This view, once described as Emergent Evolution, offers a philosophical interpretation of the universe in the light of the scientific theory of evolution. It views the universe in terms of process or becoming rather than of the static ontology of being offered by the older metaphysicians. Of special importance for this theory is the concept of genuine 'novelties' within the process whereby, as it were, the universe takes a jump forward.

A distinction is drawn between evolution as a scientific description of the process and its explanation which lies both within and outside the process, but is always related to the process. Thus Process philosophy passes easily into Process theology of which Pittenger is a distinguished exponent. While God remains the ultimate ground of the universe, the stress upon his continual relatedness to the evolutionary process, as expounded in Process thinking, leads to conclusions which differ in some respects from the traditional lines of the Christian doctrine of God.

Pittenger is therefore less suspicious than Robinson of wide-ranging metaphysical views provided that they take full account of Becoming as well as Being. He is particularly on his guard against any form of Deism, or belief in a God who is

totally uninterested in the world except as the unmoved Mover,
its final cause and ultimate explanation. He is equally opposed
to the idea of a God who 'could at best intrude into it (his
creation), deistically so to say, by an occasional miracle or by
some other such rude intervention' (*The Word Incarnate*, p.
149). Can this last phrase refer to the Incarnation as it has
been traditionally understood? He alludes with equal vigour to
Barth's heavy emphasis on divine transcendence. He writes of
the 'sheer and irrational transcendentalism of the neo-
orthodox' or Barthians (p. 153) or their 'almost spatial idea of
transcendence' (p. 177) which this seems to involve.

He warns us that the conception of God as essentially
immutable with no continuing relation to his creation may
need to be modified in the light of his primary attribute of love.
For the same reason belief in the omnipotence, omnipresence
and omniscience will need radical rethinking. We are therefore
prepared to find a strong emphasis on the immanence of God
or his continuing relation to his universe. How far these
criticisms really touch the traditional doctrine of God as both
transcendent and immanent is however more doubtful.

Yet Pittenger certainly assigns an important place to the
transcendence of God. 'God is perfect in his own
individuality—that is, there is an absolute in that God is
himself and no other' (p. 147). 'God is transcendent to his
world; he is the Holy One' (p. 176). The moral phrasing of
transcendence is closely linked to his insistence that love is the
primary attribute of God. If Pittenger hardly reaches the
robust standard of Temple's theological algebra,
'G[God]−W[the world] = G; W−G = 0', his statement is
very close to the traditional view:

> God does not need the world in order to be himself. The life
> of the triune Godhead may provide a possibility in God
> himself for realisation of the divine self-expression. This
> very self-expression which is the real nature of God in
> himself 'overspills' into creation not by some externally
> imposed necessity but by a necessity of the very nature of
> the divine being himself (p. 148).

This could stand as a description of the classical doctrine of

Creation, though the last clause recalls views of the moral necessity of Creation to God. For Pittenger, God's absoluteness or individuality must be described an an absolute relatedness.

This view of the relation between God and the world he terms *panentheism*. God is to be seen in the world or, better, the world is seen in God. God cannot be identified with the world (that would be pantheism) since he is the Supreme Creative Reality to whom all wisdom, goodness and power ultimately belong; but he is in the world since his wisdom, power and goodness are continually operative through the created order. His absolute character and his relatedness can never be divorced from each other. But is this inconsistent with a fuller (though of course non-Deistic) view of divine transcendence than Pittenger provides? The classical doctrine found less difficulty than he seems to do in speaking simultaneously of the transcendence and immanence of God or of holding together the ideas of God as both over the world and in the world or as both apart from the world and alongside the world. We must however agree with him in locating the divine immanence in the love and will of God.

For an account of divine immanence we must turn to the evolutionary world-view. Pittenger rightly distinguishes between evolution as description and evolution as explanation. For the latter there must be some grounding of the whole process in a Reality more basically real than itself. It is a Graded world order. I would even go further and speak of a graduated givenness whereby the will of God finds a richer and more open expression in the successive stages of the evolutionary process. The concept of genuine 'novelties' emergent within the process, and yet novelties in respect of the process, is crucial to his whole argument. God is at work in the whole process, yet he adapts himself (I should prefer to speak of adapting his will) to each successive stage. This accords with an old principle (which we both cordially accept) that God reveals himself and acts in the way in which it can be received (*ad modum recipientis*). This is a genuine theology of divine immanence; where Pittenger and I would probably differ is on the question whether it is reconcilable or not with the classical doctrine of divine transcendence.

This sets the stage for his Christology. On these premises a starting-point from the side of man is only to be expected. God is already purposively at work as wisdom, goodness and love within the universe. Man is a genuine 'novelty' within the process. The Incarnation then takes place in a universe which is already in some sense 'incarnational'. For Pittenger there is no decisive break, no invasion from without (the classical statement of the Incarnation), no sticking together of two utterly disparate entities (the divine and human natures of Christ) or the replacement of one entity by another (the impersonal manhood), but rather the perfectly adjusted and sufficient vehicle in and through whom the divine activity and purpose are operative in man, as man and for man. To say that the Logos became flesh or was made man is no contradiction to the emergence of this particular novelty within the process as a whole. Classically a fourfold description of the Logos was current as immanent within God (*endiathetos*), active or 'uttered' in creation (*prophorikos*), seminally present in man (*spermatikos*) and 'enmanned' (*ensarkos*). The divinity of Christ was the action of the Logos in him, the unity of divine and human in him is the coincidence of the divine and human acts. This actualisation is both from above and from below, since in this Man the fulfilment of the divine purpose is not by accident; it is of God and through the operation of God in his self-expressive Word. The image of God in man has now become the Express Image (Heb. 1.3). God lives in a human life, but living it in such a way that it is still and always human. And this true, full, genuine, complete humanity of Jesus Christ may and must be described as a Man.

So far Pittenger has produced a coherent and persuasively argued christology within the limits of Process thinking. The immanence of God must be taken seriously, though not to the complete neglect of his transcendence. Here Pittenger finds it necessary to add important qualifications. In no sense whatever does the actualisation by Christ of a human potentiality, everywhere found in men and partially realised in some of them, simply occur by some natural unfolding or by the unaided efforts of the manhood alone. It is not simply from below. It arises from above (in a different sense however from the use of this phrase in the classical view) by the divine action, the Self-Expression of God, the operation of the Word. Pittenger rejects the charge of Pelagianism or belief in an operation in which the human will is the sole agent and crowns its own endeavours. Yet both in our Lord and in the saints human activity has its part to play. Nor can the Incarnation be reduced to a special case of divine immanence. This is the burden of a long passage in *Christology Reconsidered* (p. 113) which draws a distinction between the Spirit as the principle of divine immanence and the Logos as specifically concerned with the Incarnation. Pittenger's intention is clear enough, even though the details of the passage may be more questionable.

Pittenger next turns to certain key questions in Christology in order to bring into sharper focus the difference between his restatement and the classical view. The first is the problem whether the Incarnation represents a difference in kind or in degree from the relation of God to saints and sages. The issue, though not stated in these precise terms, had already arisen in patristic times; more recently, Donald Baillie's application of the Paradox of Grace (D. M. Baillie, *God was in Christ*; Faber, 1948, pp. 114–18 and pp. 154–5) to throw light on the manner of the Incarnation was explicitly rejected by Barth as a valid analogy to the personal or hypostatic union (K. Barth, *Church Dogmatics*; T. & T. Clark, 1958 IV, 2, pp. 55–6). Barth argues that mystical union depends unilaterally on the hypostatic union and cannot be made the key to the complexities of the union of divine and human in Christ. Classical views are bound to maintain a difference in kind, while christologies which start from the side of man and speak of Christ as a man can only opt for a difference in degree. Temple (*Christus Veritas*; Macmillan, 1924 p. 147, n.l) tried to reduce the problem to logical nonsense by asking: 'Is the difference between differences of kind and differences of degree a difference of kind or a difference of degree?' Pittenger rightly regards the problem as discussable and notes that the scale in which the degree falls can be almost indefinitely extended. The absolutely unique would be completely unknowable. This is a doubtful argument for the classical view, while maintaining

that the manner of the Incarnation can only admit of partial
explanation, would agree with Pittenger that on one side it is
firmly anchored in the context of what God has done and is
doing in the universe and for men.

Pittenger next turns to the finality and uniqueness of Christ.
His fear is that too much attention to the finality of Christ may
lead to a denial of God's activity elsewhere in the universe, in
other world religions and in secular movements. But there is
nothing with which the classical view cannot cope just as
easily as can his own christology. The incarnate Logos is not
all the Logos there is. The Incarnation does not replace or
supersede the action of the seminal Logos to which he appeals.
Even his phrase 'Jesus defines but does not confine God' (*The
Word Incarnate*, p. 249) merely restates a principle common to
both schools of patristic christology, which even recurs in the
christology of Calvin. Finality as applied to Christ cannot
mean literally 'the end' for his impact still continues. The
dialectic between the final or 'once for all' and the continuing is
a major theme of the Epistle to the Hebrews. Pittenger stresses
that the finality and uniqueness of Christ must be matched by
an equal emphasis on his universality. That is certainly true
and may even be one aspect of his finality. But there is one
point well brought out in the Epistle to the Hebrews which
Pittenger seems to miss. It is the redemptive significance of
Christ which provides the context for his 'onceforallness'.
Christ is so described in the Epistles to the Hebrews as being
the objective ground for our redemption on the Godward side;
not only for Christians but for all mankind. Pittenger rejects
all transactional, legalistic, mechanical doctrines of the
Atonement without considering the abiding truth which
underlies their partial and inadequate expressions. Pittenger
prefers the terms 'definitiveness' or 'decisiveness' to 'finality' in
this context. Christ is the touchstone by which all other
insights into God must be judged. The words with which his
chapter ends are as profound as they are moving.

For us it is inconceivable that our Lord can or will be
superseded. Up until now he is unsurpassed; it is our
profound faith that he is utterly unsurpassable. For those

who follow, love and serve him, he is found to be that one in
whom Very God of Very God came in a truly human life;
and in our pettiness and sin, his Cross is found to be the
wisdom and power of God. We can only cry 'Thanks be to
God for his unspeakable gift' (p. 268).

Apart from a slight but important modification in the middle
this reads exactly like the classical christology. Those who can
take this further step have an additional reason for joining in
Pittenger's final doxology.

A similar treatment is offered of the uniqueness of Christ.
This lies not in the difference between Jesus and other men but
in what he accomplishes or achieves for other men. It is a
matter of degree rather than of kind. Taken strictly, there
cannot be degrees of uniqueness, but there is a well-established,
though looser, way of speaking of something as more or less
unique. He takes up the distinction between exclusive and
inclusive uniqueness and adopts the second sense. Christ is
unique as the Representative Man; the Second Adam who
includes others in his decisive role. None of this is of course
disputed by the classical Christology but it would assert
exclusive uniqueness as well. One man in human history was
the Son of God incarnate. Pittenger would argue that a
doctrine of the exclusive uniqueness of Christ would lift him
altogether out of the context of the divine-human relationship
as men otherwise know and share it and make him a 'bolt from
the blue' or the result of a 'rude intervention' from outside the
process. Classical views maintain that apart from exclusive
uniqueness the divine solidarity of the incarnate Lord would
lack one important element, the personal assumption by God
the Logos of a complete human nature on his descent into
human life for us men and for our salvation. This is the vital
difference between such a Christology as that of Pittenger and
classical views.

We can now turn to some more general criticisms of
Pittenger's position. He cannot fairly be accused of neglecting
the transcendence of God. His panentheism has the aim of
relating the universe as closely to God as possible without
denying divine transcendence. This may well be a necessary

protest against the unduly heavy accent on the transcendence
of God in Deism and possibly some tendencies in Barth. Yet
by reason of the problems to which it addresses itself, his own
approach, while rightly redressing the balance in favour of
divine immanence, tends to underestimate the full self-
existence of God apart from his 'absolute relatedness' and the
complementary truth of his divine 'overagainstness'. I am not
suggesting that theology should 'hop on the other foot for a
change' but that it should walk steadily on two feet. For this
the supranaturalist frame is as essential as a realistic
assessment of God in relation to his universe.

Process theology offers an interpretation of divine
immanence within an evolutionary view of the universe. That
is clear gain. But is it equally well adapted to express the
speciality of the Incarnation? The evocative idea of an
'incarnational' universe may conceal an important ambiguity.
If it means a universe of such a character as to support and to
provide the groundwork for an Incarnation; well and good.
Divine immanence prepares the way or sets the stage for what
is to occur within it. God always speaks and acts relevantly to
the recipients of his disclosure in word and deed. But if the
phrase implies that the universe by its own character
determines the structure of the Incarnation, then this is more
doubtful.

Pittenger expressly rejects the criticism that he is reducing
the Incarnation to a special case of divine immanence. Yet
perhaps inevitably the fruitful idea of man as a genuine novelty
within the process, yet arising from the process, 'overspills'
into his thinking about the Incarnation. His carefully guarded
preference for a degree Christology tells in the same direction.
Is the Incarnation on his premises more than a 'starred'
novelty, in the way in which some universities leave room in
their class lists for a 'starred first'? Does his view leave room
for the possibility of an event different from the process and yet
relevantly related to the process? Father Lionel Thornton in
his book *The Incarnate Lord* (Longman, 1928) adopted a
similar philosophical framework to that of Pittenger but found
it necessary at this point of the Incarnation to desert it in order
to provide more adequately for the conditions of the

Incarnation. Pittenger naturally regrets that Thornton did not follow out the logical conclusions to which his general approach ought to have led him. His change of front indicated a feeling of disquiet about the adequacy of Process thinking to express all that needs to be said about the Incarnation. Was this merely a failure of nerve on Thornton's part or a recognition of the inadequacy of his philosophical framework at this precise point?

Process thinking naturally leads to an optimistic world-view even if it is not necessarily committed to the earlier facile evolutionary optimism. Pittenger devotes a whole chapter in *Christology Reconsidered* (pp. 45–65) to the subject of 'Jesus and human sin'. He indignantly repudiates the charge of Pelagianism brought against him by some critics. The actualisation of human potentialities does not come about through unaided human effort even if man must play his part. The divine intention for man has been accompanied by a human distortion or deviation of aims. Sin is the refusal to play one's part in the total expression of love-in-action; a saying 'No' to the cosmic love which seeks to express itself in and through man for the fulfilment of his own potentiality and for making actual the divine love which is God himself. Sin therefore is an absence, even a negation, of love and only love can redeem man from sin. Although in his true human reality each man is not a sinner, empirically we know well that he is a sinner. Further his true realisation is of grace and not of works; since he cannot become in full freedom the expressive agent for the highest and deepest Love, God himself, except through dependence upon that highest and deepest Love.

This view lacks neither truth nor nobility. It claims support from the biblical view of man as made in the image of God and from the original meaning of the word normally used for sin in the New Testament (*hamartia*, or 'missing the mark'), though Pittenger is less happy about the corresponding word 'transgression' (*parabasis*) which implies the breach of a God-given law. He appeals to Augustine ('Man is made towards God') against Augustinianism and rejects the traditional Western estimate of man and sin as Manichaean or dualist in tendency. Barthians blacken human nature intolerably. Clearly

Pittenger adopts a relatively light, though not a Pelagian, view
of sin. We miss the notes of fallenness, alienation and
estrangement from God which Tillich urged so strongly.
Naturally Pittenger can find no place in his Christology for a
divine rescue operation breaking into the process at cost from
above. His preference for the Scotist view, that the Incarnation
would have occurred even apart from human sin, against the
Thomist alternative which links it directly with sin and its
remedy, is significant. Objective views of the Atonement are
dismissed by Pittenger as legalistic, transactional and
mechanical on the score of the imagery in which they have
often been expressed. He emphasises splendidly the action of
'Christ in us' without seeing that its precondition is 'Christ for
us'. A less light view of sin would lead to the requirement of a
more radical descent of God into the evolutionary process to
meet our needs. For the determination of the special conditions
of the Incarnation the predicament of man in the process is no
less important than his place within the process.

The advantages of christologies from the side of man are not
negligible. They can assert the full solidarity of the incarnate
Lord with us without a trace of psychological docetism or an
appeal to the difficult notion of the 'impersonal manhood'.
They offer a meaningful account of the growth and the
temptations of our Lord. To Temple's test-question: 'If the
Logos were taken away from the incarnate Lord, what would
be left?' they answer unequivocally: 'a complete man'. They
make the human Jesus a partner, though a junior partner, with
the Logos, in the work of redemption. They can provide an
indefinitely great degree of difference between the incarnate
Lord and other men. They can relate the Incarnation directly
to divine immanence and to a modern world-view of the
evolutionary type. They can claim a measure of support in the
Dualist Christology of the age of the fathers. The involvement
of God the Logos in the Incarnation is not denied but restated
in terms of activity, a union in love, without recourse to what
they regard as the static and outdated forms of the older
ontology.

Yet there are corresponding disadvantages. The divine
initiative (though not denied) is gravely weakened by the

rejection of the supranaturalist frame. The divine condescension expressed in terms of a divine descent is notably absent from this type of Christology. The idea of a divine rescue operation implied in objective views of the Atonement is necessarily absent. The firm personal centre of the incarnate Lord is shifted from God the Logos to the man Jesus with a consequent weakening of the divine involvement as 'God's presence and his very self'. The notion of a relational union, however attractively presented in moral or spiritual terms, lacks a firm ontological grounding and stops short of the ultimate target of a personal or hypostatic union.

Christology from the side of man raises three questions in the minds of those who cannot accept its adequacy. Despite all that it can and does provide, is it working a dimension short? Is it capable of providing the full measure of divine self-involvement in the Incarnation? Can its relational bond of union between the Logos and the human Jesus provide sufficiently for the union between God and man which the Incarnation involves and our redemption requires? These are certainly not negligible issues.

6 Christology and related doctrines

ONE of the difficulties about Christology is the number of related issues in other fields of Christian doctrine. This is hardly surprising since the coherence of Christian doctrine is one test of its truth. In this chapter we shall be concerned with the doctrines of the Trinity and of Redemption though the latter will also call for a look at the doctrine of Grace.

I

At first sight the doctrine of the Trinity might seem to be free-standing and unlikely to be affected by developments in Christology. In the fourth and fifth centuries the protagonists of the rival christologies were firmly orthodox in their Trinitarian theology by Nicene standards. Their slight divergences, chiefly in the use of technical terms, did not arise from their Christology. The solidarity of God the Logos with the Father expressed by the *Homoousion* (of one substance) was common ground. Their differences arose from the way in which they saw the relation between the Logos and the humanity within the incarnate life. Monists regarded the Logos as the personal centre and his humanity as the circumference through which he touched human life. Dualists thought of the divinity and the humanity as the two foci of an ellipse. The Monists laid great emphasis on the divine descent of the Logos into incarnate existence. The Dualist starting-point was the full co-presence of the two natures within the incarnate life. In neither case was the doctrine of the Trinity affected in the slightest. The Arian confusion of the two doctrines was sufficient warning not to fall into the same pitfall again.

Yet historically in the development of Christian doctrine a connection between the two fields certainly existed. The doctrine of the Trinity can partly be regarded as an extended doctrinal inference from the two great New Testament facts: the centrality of Christ and the experience of the Holy Spirit. In the earliest centuries the main weight of development towards a Trinitarian doctrine was borne by the relation between the Father and the Son or the Logos, while the doctrine of the Holy Spirit was developed as a kind of tailpiece or appendix between the Councils of Nicaea (325) and Constantinople (381).

Within the New Testament itself, as we have seen, the watershed of the Resurrection led to the discovery by the Church of the continuing impact of the Risen Lord, different in idiom but identical in impact with his fellowship with his disciples during his earthly life. His 'post-earthly existence' led to the further inference of his pre-existence clarified by means of the Old Testament concepts of the Wisdom and the Word. Originally personifications, they had received sharper definition in the Judaism of the Dispersion largely under the impact of Greek philosophy but, above all, through their association with the Risen Christ. His centrality to Redemption was linked with his participation in Creation. Christ in the Christian and the Church became extended to Christ in the universe, the cosmic Christ. The tentatively expressed acclamations of Christ as God needed further exploration and thus began the longer journey which led to full affirmation of the Nicene Creed 'of one substance with the Father'.

While however historically the doctrine of the Trinity represented an extended inference from the fact of Christ and the work of the Holy Spirit, it is even more important to remember that the Church believed that the new doctrine represented the best human approximation to the truth about God on the basis of the data of the New Testament.

Different versions of the doctrine of the Trinity were attempted before they were adjudged inadequate and either outgrown or condemned as heretical. The first, called Modalism or Sabellianism—after Sabellius, its most systematic exponent in the third century—held that the threeness of the one God could best be described as modes or manifestations, whether simultaneous or successive. God was essentially or basically one but he manifested himself in three ways. This version was tried and found wanting since it led to inconsequences, both theological and christological. It offered a picture of God who was everything by turns and nothing for long, 'a turncoat deity' (Tertullian) or (in the more precise language of Basil in the fourth century) 'a God who transformed himself to meet the changing needs of the world'. Early Modalists maintained that the Father became incarnate as the Son, and therefore suffered. It was therefore called Patripassianism on the ground that it 'crucified the Father' (Tertullian). To speak of the Incarnation of God without further qualification is, then as now, an inaccurate use of language. In the long run it was a more adequate and God-worthy inference from the biblical data to claim that God manifested himself in three ways because he was already in some sense threefold than to stop short at the seemingly more modest statement that God, while being essentially one, allowed himself to be approached in three ways.

A second exploration, which was for some time widely current, was the theory of Economic or Functional Trinitarianism. This view agreed with Modalism that God was essentially one, but gave a richer content to the threeness of the Godhead. In the course of his creative and redemptive purposes for the world the one God 'uttered' or extrapolated the Word and the Spirit as economies or functional activities. Once they were brought into existence they continued as differentiated beings. In one late fourth-century form of the theory, the moment of their origin as independent economies was specifically dated, Creation in the case of the Son and the Inbreathing of the Spirit into the disciples (John 20.22) in the case of the Spirit. Since logically their independent existence was inseparably linked with their functions, it was natural to infer that, when the world came to an end, they should be resumed back into the unitary glory of the Father. This was deduced from 1 Cor. 15.28. In this developed form the whole process of the extension and retraction of the Godhead was described in terms used in Greek medicine for the dilation and contraction of the human heart. The Trinitarian episode therefore resembled a rhythmic heart-beat of the divine life. In its earlier and less sophisticated form this theory had the merit of keeping more closely in touch with Salvation History as the Bible depicts it, the Logos as the counsellor of the Father at Creation and the prime agent in the Incarnation and the Spirit outpoured at Pentecost upon the Church. It had however two fatal objections. It confused the operations of the divine persons towards creation (what was later described as their 'missions') with their inner relationship to the Father (later called their 'processions'). It failed to discern that what God does, he antecedently is; or, to put the point slightly differently, his functional activities can be regarded as a reliable pointer to his inner being as well as to his dispensation for his creatures in time. The progress beyond Modalism was therefore not as marked as might have been thought.

The Church was therefore led beyond these two phrasings of the doctrine of the Trinity to a full immanent or essential Trinity. The threefold manifestation of God or his threefold economy or functional activity towards creation was taken as a real pointer towards his inner and essential being. God manifested himself or acted in three ways because he was already threefold in himself without ceasing to be one God. A differentiated or expanded monotheism at this level alone could satisfy the necessary inferences from the biblical data with regard to the Son and the Holy Spirit. Against his Sabellian opponents Basil speaks of modes of being as against mere modes of manifestation. Only a metaphysical or ontological scaffolding could in the long run make adequate provision for Christian monotheism.

Clearly a Christology from the side of God has no motive to modify or abandon this framework. A firm Logos centre in the incarnate Lord requires an equally strong doctrine of the Trinity. Some modern christologies from the side of man again report 'No change'. Donald Baillie, whose christology in his book *God was in Christ* bears a general family resemblance to the opinions discussed in the previous chapter, shows no tendency to modify the traditional doctrine. John Knox (*The Humanity and Divinity of Christ*, p. 109) explicitly asks the questions: 'What happens on this view [of pre-existence] to the doctrine of the Trinity?', and replies (rather surprisingly):

> Nothing at all. Any doctrine of the Incarnation must
> presuppose the Trinity—or, at any rate, some complexity (if
> that can be the word)—in God. In no serious theology,
> ancient or modern, has the Pre-existent Christ been
> identified with God, simply and absolutely.

If this statement is too brief to be altogether lucid, its intention
at least is clear. Pittenger's chapter on 'The Incarnation and
the Trinity' (*The Word Incarnate*, pp. 215–35) is a pleasure to
read. It is a fresh statement of the classical doctrine which
raises few problems.

The situation is different with other writers. Robinson is
prepared to jettison some essential elements in the doctrine of
the Trinity: the individuality of God the Son and the Eternal
Generation of the Son by the Father. This arises mainly from
his reductionist exegesis of the New Testament and his reading
of the implication of Knox's interpretation of pre-existence. In
his essay on Christology in *Soundings* (Cambridge, 1962, pp.
165 and 171) Bishop Montefiore advocates a retreat from an
Essential Trinitarianism to a more Economic approach:
'Instead of defining the Essential Trinity of three Persons, we
must content ourselves with the experience of the divine
activity in three modes.' 'By asserting an "economic Trinity"
and by refusing to go beyond the known to the unknown, we
do not imperil the Unity of God.' He is not of course
discussing the doctrine of the Trinity as an end in itself, but
arguing for the use of 'activity' as a key feature both in
Christology and Trinitarianism. He must certainly not be
debited with the more striking features of the Patristic form of
the doctrine. Like most recent champions of a christology from
the side of man he supports a reinterpretation of the older
ontological categories in terms of activity. His proposal at
least has the merit of logical consistency in using the same
concept as a master-theme in both fields.

Montefiore has, it seems, three objections to the classical
doctrine, of which the third is probably the one on which he
lays the greatest stress. The first objection is that the full
doctrine of the Trinity imperils the unity of God. But this is to

ignore the role of the *Homoousion* as the sheet-anchor of the divine unity. All later explorations of the divine plurality took this for granted and fell consciously and deliberately within the limits which it set. The question which the Fathers both in the East and the West were asking after Nicaea was 'Given the unity in substance of the Godhead what place can be assigned to the plurality of persons'? The second objection, implied rather than stated, is the allegedly static character of the metaphysical terms in which the doctrine was expressed. Here we may recall that Basil clarifies the word 'person' in the accepted formula as 'three energies or activities'. He is not 'beating a retreat' from 'person' to 'activity' but selecting one aspect of being a person to make its meaning clear. Montefiore's real objection however appears to be that in speaking of the inner and essential being of God the classical doctrine goes beyond what is knowable by man. For him the transcendent is the unknown 'just as "I" am transcendent of my consciousness'.

Whether the psychological analogy works or not, he is drawing too sharp a contrast between the transcendence of God (God as he is in himself) who is in principle unknown and his immanent activity which can be recognised and known. But Christian theology has always sought to avoid the danger of setting as it were two Gods in opposition: the hidden God and the revealed God; and positively has claimed that his transcendence is of one piece with his immanence. What God has revealed of himself in activity or in speech is a reliable clue to what he is in himself. This finds expression in the sound principle that 'what God does, he antecendently is' or, as the Scholastics put it, 'Operation follows being' (*operari sequitur esse*). Even in constructing the doctrine of an immanent or essential Trinity Christian theology has never claimed to comprehend God (short of the Beatific Vision) but only to offer the best human approximation to the truth about him. Montefiore stops short at function or operation; Christian thinking has gone further and with the necessary provisos and qualifications dared to speak of the inner and essential being of God. To move one step further back in the development of the doctrine marks a retreat or a reduction rather than a restatement. The doctrine of an essential or Immanent Trinity provides a fuller basis for what needs to be said about God, whether as a reflection of the biblical data or as an extended inference from them, rather than a theology which stops short at the divine functions, operations and activities.

II

An even closer relationship exists between the doctrines of the Incarnation and Redemption. This is inevitable because the Person and Work of Christ cannot be isolated from each other. Although in the Patristic period the doctrine of Redemption lagged behind the doctrine of the Incarnation, the need for christologies to provide adequately for the conditions of Redemption was widely recognised. No christology could be a serious candidate for truth which failed to make sense theologically of the fact of Redemption. The effect of this correlation between the two doctrines on the assessment of the human experiences of the incarnate Lord has already been traced in sufficient detail. It only remains to summarise the issues on both side which appeared to be at stake. The first can be defined as Transmissibility as against Relevance. For the Monist, unless the incarnate Lord was a divinely centred Person, the Redemption which he brought could not avail for all mankind. For the Dualist, unless Christ was a man like ourselves in all respects, sin only excepted, his Redemption could not be relevant or speak to our condition. The Monist therefore considered his humanity, whatever its extent, as the human conditioning of the incarnate Logos; the Dualist regarded the 'assumed man' as virtually a 'junior partner' to the Logos in the work of redemption. The Monist described the process of being redeemed in terms of deification or divinisation, whether interpreted more or less strictly in ontological terms, or mystically and sacramentally, as an extension of the Pauline concept of incorporation into the Body of Christ. Language of this type was deeply suspected by the Dualists who preferred to speak about our participation in the death and resurrection of the 'assumed man'.

The doctrine of Grace and the divide in Christian spirituality to which it gave rise is closely linked to the doctrine of Redemption. Here the lead was taken by the West in the controversy between Augustine and Pelagius. The East remained somewhat on the sidelines. This was in no sense a debate about Christology and only affects the doctrine of the Person from its repercussions in the area of Redemption. While historical connections between Pelagian doctrines of Man and of Grace and the Dualist tradition in Christology cannot be dismissed, they have not yet been convincingly demonstrated. The oft-quoted judgement of Bishop Gore that 'the Nestorian Christ is the fitting Saviour of Pelagian man' merely calls attention to a general similarity of approach.

The fundamental difference between the two protagonists is summarised by the contrast between Monergism (Augustine) and Synergism (Pelagius). The former insists upon the sole action of God in the life of Grace, while the latter maintains a kind of partnership between God and man. In one passage Paul seems to put the two standpoints together without finding any need to arbitrate between them: 'Work out your own salvation in fear and trembling [synergism] for it is God which worketh in you [monergism] both to will and to do according to his good pleasure' (Phil. 2.12–13). It should be made clear that the champions of both views tended to overrun their primary objectives. Many of the more extreme Augustinian positions failed to commend themselves to later centuries, while Pelagius represented an extreme form of Synergism. Other Western theologians with an untarnished reputation for orthodoxy combined the central insights of Augustine with Synergistic elements. It was in fact a modified Augustinianism which finally prevailed. The contrast pointed out here nevertheless remains valid.

For Augustine Grace is essentially a divine act which extends throughout the whole of the Christian life. Whether it is begun, continued or ended, it is all of God and therefore of Grace. Man can never take the initiative with God and all that he contributes is his great and bitter need. Grace is therefore regarded as powerful rescue; and the more powerful its operation, the more truly it is Grace, though Augustine just stops short of calling it irresistible. For him grace is primarily grace of redemption or saving grace, though he would not have

denied that creation itself was an act of grace. The predicament
to which God addressed himself in grace was the fact and the
consequences of human sin. Augustine paints a dark picture of
human sin which is a radical surd in human nature. Guilt,
transgression and disobedience strike closer to the heart of the
matter than a missing of the mark or a failure to realise the
divine purpose of love. Man is morally and spiritually
bankrupt before God, though we need not trace here the stages
of the argument by which Augustine reached this conclusion.
His doctrine of the Fall, of original sin and guilt, represents a
separate topic and forms the most disputable part of his
treatment.

The question which most directly concerns us is what place
Augustine can assign to human freedom in the light of his
emphasis on Grace as powerful rescue and his pessimistic
reading of the human situation. Earlier in his career he had
defended freedom against the pessimistic dualism of the
Manichees. Now in his debate with Pelagius he found it
necessary to reduce its potentiality considerably. Indeed he
was much embarrassed in the course of the controversy when
Pelagius quoted the earlier Augustine against the later. No
man likes to be quoted as an authority against himself! It was
at this point that his refutation of Pelagian opinions turned into
an attack upon Pelagius himself. He explains his change of
front, at least to his own satisfaction, with the words 'I
laboured hard and earnestly for free will, but grace won the
day.' The truth is that for Augustine Grace and Freedom
belonged to the same field of forces and were therefore in
tension, if not also in opposition, to each other. His general
view is that, while man has retained free will as the capacity of
turning intention into action—good, bad or indifferent—he
has totally lost the true freedom to live according to the will of
God 'Whose service is perfect freedom'. The door here is
opened by Grace and Grace alone. This central insight of
Augustine may well be truer than much of the detail of his
massive, if ruthless, system.

The starting-point of Pelagius could not have been more
different. Theologically (and perhaps temperamentally) he had
a more optimistic estimate of human nature than Augustine.

Much of his pastoral counselling, contained in his moral treatises, was an attempt to stimulate lazy or wordly Christians to greater moral effort. A prayer of Augustine which was reported to him, 'Give what thou dost command and command what thou wilt', seemed to him destructive of moral effort. While not every opinion of his followers can be debited to Pelagius, he seems to have been a more substantial theological figure than has commonly been believed. His starting-point was the grace of Creation: 'God saw that it was good'. The image of God in man might become tarnished but could not be obliterated. There was nothing that could not be rubbed off. Man was certainly not sinful by nature (that would be Manicheeism) but only by reason of sins which he had actually committed himself. While Pelagius accepted the practice of Infant Baptism as conveying membership of the Church and the pledge of an eternal inheritance, it could not transmit remission of sins since the infant had not as yet committed any sinful acts.

Following Paul, Pelagius marked three stages in the spiritual history of mankind, centred in Adam, Moses and Christ respectively. From Adam to Moses man relied on his nature, the image of God in which he was originally created. To restore this image after it had become tarnished Moses received the Law as moral guidelines for a right relationship with God. When this proved too weak for its purpose Christ came with his gospel which was virtually a republication of the law of man's own nature. At every stage of this history of salvation sinless men could be found. What God provided was conditioned by what in his integrity and freedom needed and could receive. Although occasionally Pelagius can write that we can act 'more easily' through Grace, his normal view is that it operates through precept and (with Christ) by example. The Pauline antithesis between the Law and the gospel is completely ignored. What God provides are the guidelines. It is for man in his freedom to make the appropriate effort for successful living.

If Augustine seems to overstate man's predicament, Pelagius never gets within striking distance of seeing its true dimension. While at some points Pelagius may provide a necessary 'Yes but' to the detail of Augustine's system, there is no question which of the two had the deeper insight into man's need and God's answer in Redemption. Both men however shared the same assumption of possible collision between Grace and freedom but took different steps to avoid it. Pelagius narrows the scope of Grace to provide more adequately for the integrity and freedom of man. Augustine restricts freedom, to the greater glory of Grace. Pelagius, who believed in the sovereign and unimpaired freedom of the human will, looks to Grace primarily for light on a road which we can and must travel ourselves. For Augustine, Grace is first and foremost a powerful rescue which God, 'seeing that we have no power of ourselves to help ourselves', alone can supply. The priority of Grace at every stage of the Christian life reflects the divine initiative. Pelagius is so afraid of setting up an imbalance between Grace and free will that he misses completely the glory of Redemption. Neither, of course, could appeal to the modern concept of personality which leaves room for the powerful impact of one person on another without infringing the liberty of either.

These two approaches to the doctrine of Grace issue in two different patterns of the Christian life. Monergism results in a life of dependence upon God to which man through Grace must continually respond. Synergism considers man a veritable partner with God, playing his own subordinate but indispensable part in the adventure of discipleship. Once again, a partial reconciliation can be found in human personal relations. This can be illustrated from the relation of student and tutor. A grateful pupil may visit his tutor after a successful performance in his examinations and make the Monergist-type statement 'I could not have done it without you' or 'I owe it all to you'. And this may well be true because without the guidance and inspiration of his tutor the student might well have been an 'unguided missile'. But if he is wise as well as learned, the tutor will reply 'Nonsense, you did it yourself', and this will be true as well for it was the student who did the work and wrote the paper. Every happily married man will be able to carry this analogy a good deal further for himself. Personal relations at any deep level involve both mutual dependence and shared human effort. In Christian discipleship those who think most readily of their dependence upon God also find themselves committed in practice to a life of active service, while those who start with the idea of active partnership with God will not be able to proceed very far without realising their dependence upon God. The point of entry and balance of emphasis are certainly different, but they may not ultimately be incompatible. This measure of reconcilation between rival views may certainly work in the mapwork of the Christian life and even possibly in the doctrine of Grace as the divine provision for Christian existence. The two approaches here correspond closely enough, though they are not identical with the two early schools of Christology which focused attention upon a Logos-centred Person on the one hand, and the 'assumed man' as virtually a co-partner with the Logos in the work of Redemption on the other.

The inference from a God-centred Redemption to a Christology from the side of God seems almost irresistible but it has been strongly challenged by exponents of the opposite standpoint. The first criticism arises from the concept of deification which was regarded by Cyril and other Greek fathers as the corollary of their Logos-centred christology. Those who are redeemed through the agency of a Logos-centred Person are themselves 'divinised'. The facts here are not in dispute, but different interpretations of their significance for Christology are admissible. The connection, though natural for Cyril to make, is more accidental than essential, a deduction from his Christology which could well stand without it. If deification is understood in an ontological way, then it attempts to leap the gap between the Creator and the creature and forgets that even in the experience of Redemption we remain obstinately and irrevocably human. If it is used in a mystical and sacramental sense, then it may merely be the equivalent of the Pauline concept of incorporation in Christ and our adoptive sonship of God through Christ. Mystical identification differs considerably from ontological solidarity. It will still seem to many to 'jump the points' but in a much less exceptionable manner.

This is not however the sole context against which a God-centred Redemption can be expressed. There is the Augustinian view of a powerful rescue operation initiated from the side of God and demanding the fullest measure of divine involvement. Professor Maurice Wiles (*Christ, Faith and History*; Cambridge, 1972, pp. 8–10) urges a reinterpretation of the whole complex Creation–Fall–Incarnation on the ground that in classical theology the three belong together and the almost complete abandonment of belief in the Fall as in principle a historically dateable event must lead to a reassessment of the whole framework.

The comments of Professor Baelz in the same book (pp. 19–22) are well worth consulting. While with Creation and the Incarnation we are concerned with the manner or structure of divine action, 'If God is absent anywhere, he is surely absent from the Fall.' It makes no significant difference whether the Fall is regarded as an event or as a parable of man's fallenness, alienation or estrangement. The central insight of Augustine into man's predicament and God's provision to meet it stands fast. The detail of the Augustinian position may here, as elsewhere, need considerable revision. The dark view of sin and the extent of the divine involvement to meet it cannot lightly be dismissed.

Pittenger accuses Barthians (and others who accept Augustine's diagnosis) of blackening human nature unduly and of tending dangerously towards a fundamental dualism of the Manichean type. This charge was brought against Augustine even in his own day. Unfortunately there is much evidence, not least in modern times, to support a dark view of sin and its outcome, which still makes Augustine a more reliable guide than many more favourable estimates of man, whether Pelagian or not. Pittenger, while readily admitting that empirically we are all sinners, protests against any view which makes sin an essential part of human nature. But that is not of the essence of the Augustinian contract. Aquinas, for example, rejects views of sin which regard it as an essential part of human nature and yet he recognises the need for a radical Redemption from the side of God. Pittenger rejects doctrines of the Atonement which see in Christ the objective ground of our redemption as external, transactional and legal but this

criticism confuses the language in which a doctrine has
historically been expressed with its underlying meaning and
intention. 'Christ for us' is the necessary precondition of
'Christ in us' if our Redemption is to be firmly rooted and
solidly grounded in the divine act. The one depends upon the
other and cannot replace it in our thinking about the
Atonement. However movingly Pittenger expresses the
redemptive action of Christ in us, there is a missing previous
step which leaves his argument incomplete.

Christologies from the side of man claim to provide
adequately for the needs of Redemption. Only if the humanity
of Christ is full, complete and individual could Redemption be
relevant to us. The restoration or redirection of the human will
is an important ingredient in the experience of being redeemed
and for this a human will in Christ is essential. Their doctrine
of Grace in so far as it is expressed is fundamentally Synergist,
even though it need not be Pelagian, and its view of sin is
normally light rather than dark. Their christology is based on a
moral and spiritual unity between God the Logos and a Jesus
who was never and had never been other than a man, and this
can supply all that can legitimately be asked for the purposes
of Redemption. If we appeal to 'God in Christ' and can say
divine things about Jesus, that will be enough. While admitting
an almost uncalculable difference in degree between Christ and
ourselves, the 'paradox of Grace', in Donald Baillie's phrase,
can throw much-needed light on the doctrine of the
Incarnation. This is certainly neither a negligible nor unworthy
view which can be attractively presented.

A christology from the side of God can reply that it has
gone far to maintain a full, complete and individual humanity
without taking the final step which the rival christology finds
essential. After much initial hesitation the existence of a
human soul in Christ was completely accepted. The last
refinement of its development after Chalcedon declared
unambiguously for a human will in Christ. With its strong
emphasis on a Logos-centred Person and its use of an allegedly
static ontology which has been accused of neglecting or
undervaluing relations we might have expected the opposite
conclusion, either on the ground of the unity of will between

the Father and his incarnate Son or of the inclusion of the will
in the *hypostasis* which was restricted to that of God the
Logos, much as William Temple was later to identify will and
personality. Evidently the emphasis on will in the Dualist
tradition, as much for redemptive as for christological reasons,
had not gone unheeded; by this time, if not earlier, will was
included in nature. Even more important, Barth was merely
following the classical tradition both in West and East in
claiming that the humanity of Christ was a complete,
individual humanity despite the absence of an independent
hypostasis. While this does not satisfy the requirements of a
modern christology from the side of man, it is not always
recognised how far the classical tradition went in this direction.

Normally the doctrine of Grace associated with the classical
Christology is Monergist in emphasis without necessarily
denying some Synergistic elements in a Christian life of
responsive dependence upon God; and its doctrine of sin is
dark both in its character and results. As the divine remedy for
sin the Incarnation requires a fuller divine initiative and a
deeper divine involvement than in the rival tradition. 'Christ
for us' is the precondition and ground of our salvation and is
therefore prior to 'Christ in us', the fruit of our redemption and
the hope of our future glory. Christ the Redeemer is the divine
agent in a rescue operation from the side of God on behalf of
man in his fallenness, alienation and estrangement. But it is
also a relevant redemption since it is achieved through the
assumption by the Logos of a complete and individual, though
not a theoretically detachable, humanity. The Incarnation is
therefore unique in kind, and not merely in degree, however
incalculable in practice the degree may be reckoned. There is
certainly a paradox of Grace, the 'I, yet not I' of Pauline
theology; but the paradox of the Incarnation, 'The Word made
flesh' on which it depends is not only far greater but positively
unique, and the one paradox depends unilaterally on the other.
Barth's criticism of Baillie's use of mystical union as an
adequate account of the Incarnation is reasonable and just.
Again, as Barth clearly saw, the 'Homecoming of the Son of
Man' would be a dimension short without the previous 'Way of
the Son of God into a Far Country', and the homecoming of

the sons of men through redemption depends not upon the former alone but on both taken together.

It seems therefore on grounds of the correlation of Redemption and the Incarnation that a christology from the side of God is greatly to be preferred to a christology from the side of man. It is not only in Christology proper that the rival tradition is working a dimension short.

7 Jesus Christ true God and true Man

THE Incarnation is both the self-disclosure of God in and to man and the redemptive action of God through man on behalf of men. But what bearing has this on the structure of the Person of Christ and what are its implications for Christology? We have examined in sufficient detail for our purpose the two main types of Christology which have contributed to the elucidation of the problem. We must in conclusion sort out the principal ingredients of Christology in the light of our discussion and sum up the results which appear to emerge.

Both types of Christology agree that a double solidarity exists in the incarnate Lord, both with the Father and with ourselves; they express it in different ways and give it a different weighting. Its weakest form is the two stories which can be told about the same fact, the human Jesus. The first lies within the world of observable and empirical facts; the second concerns its meaning and significance, and is mythological in form and character. The problem is that both stories do not belong to the realm of thought and have no clear dovetail into each other. In the absence of any suitable overlap between the two, it is difficult to see why the second should be worth hearing or continue to be told. Robinson's interpretation of the double solidarity as two levels of understanding Jesus is more positive and explicit. Jesus is 'the human face of God', both 'the Man for others' and 'a window into God at work'. He is 'God for us', 'the man who lived God'. This admits of a fuller solidarity on both sides, but the accent falls heavily on the side of man. There is a pressure to say divine things about Jesus which can and must be satisfied, but it can only be understood as a second level of interpreting Jesus. Whatever is said from

124

the divine side must be capable of being related to a particular man, Jesus the Christ. The divine initiative represents his calling as the man of God's own choosing marking him off from any ordinary or routine man. The divine involvement is interpreted as his utter transparency to God in the depths of his being without detriment to his essential humanity. His divinity must therefore find expression in functional or relational terms.

The classical statement tries to provide a more solid ground in its doctrine of the two natures. His divine nature gives the fullest possible grounding for his solidarity with God; his solidarity with ourselves is satisfied by his human nature which is in principle complete. But it adds, not as a rider but as a complementary truth, the union of the two natures in a single Person of which the ultimate subject is God the Son. The divine nature is therefore not something which the incarnate Person has, but what he essentially is; the humanity is something which he assumes in addition to what he is. The double solidarity is certainly present but, while the divine solidarity is fully provided, it has historically found itself in greater difficulties on the human side. In the earlier stages of the development of this tradition the humanity was considered primarily as the necessary conditioning of God the Logos inherent in the very act of becoming Incarnate. The existence of a human soul in Christ was not an automatic starting-point but a hardly-won and possibly a reluctant conclusion, imposed upon it either by the logical extremities of one of its own supporters, Apollinarius, or by the rubbing off of some of the insights of its opponents. Even after its explicit acceptance some leading Monist christologians hardly know what to do with it, and traces of psychological docetism survived for many centuries. The human will of Christ was pencilled in as the final stage of the evolution of the classical position. Even when the human nature was described as individual as well as complete, it still lacked its own *hypostasis*. It was not regarded as 'independently represented', but received its personal centre within that of God of Logos. For the classical statement the incarnate Lord was both 'true God' and 'true man' but the two solidarities, though both present, do not carry equal weight.

The second problem is even more difficult for both traditions

to handle. It concerns the personal centre of the incarnate
Lord. Christologies from the side of God accentuate God the
Son or the Logos as the ultimate subject of the Incarnation;
christologies from the side of man emphasise the full
individuality of the human Jesus, described without reserve
and hesitation as a man, as the immediate subject of the
incarnate life.

The classical statement which starts from the side of God
asserts (with Barth) that only God can reveal God, and (with
Augustine) that only God can redeem and rescue man. The
divine initiative involves a divine descent; a divine inbreaking.
The divine involvement is put at its maximum. God the Son or
Logos is the ultimate subject of the incarnate life and retains
the divine nature which is essentially his. Only so can this
Revelation of God have its ultimate guarantee and authority.
Only so can the Redemption which he came to bring be a fully
divine act transmissible to all men at all times. Yet his
humanity must also be involved if his Revelation is not to be a
mere self-display of God to himself but readily available to
those to whom it is addressed, and if his Redemption is to
speak to the condition of those for whom it was achieved. Both
Revelation and Redemption require the presence of the 'true
God', but by the same token the incarnate Person must also be
'true man'. To describe the union of God and man in one
divinely centred Person only ontological thought-forms like
'substance', 'nature' and 'Person' can suffice. But here the most
serious difficulty of the classical statement arises. A personal
union of this type is certainly unique, and adequate parallels or
even reliable analogies cannot be expected. The first attempt to
meet it was the doctrine of the *Enhypostasia* or the concept of
God the Logos acting in a double capacity as the immediate
subject of the divine nature, and (at a lower level of potency) of
the human nature as well. This is a perfectly tenable position,
given the intellectual background and conceptual tools of the
classical period. That it is difficult to envisage is only to be
expected if the resultant Person is unique. So far attempts to
restate it in psychological or other terms have proved
unconvincing. Kenoticism takes a further step to ease the
problem with its suggestion that by the masking or retraction

of some divine attributes during the Incarnation, God the Logos allowed the measures of the humanity to prevail over himself, and lives in and through it even in his relations to his Father. This is a difficult but not impossible conception which, while retaining the thrust of a christology from the side of God, clarifies to some extent what this appears to involve.

The opposite tradition in Patristic times took the existence of a human soul for granted and gave an indispensable place to a human will in its scheme of Redemption. The human nature, often robustly described as 'a man', is virtually a 'junior partner' with the Logos in the work of Redemption. While indignantly repudiating a doctrine of 'Two Sons' or a double personal centre in Christ, it preferred to use relational terms to express the conjunction of the Logos with the assumed man. It is not altogether clear how the real subject of the incarnate experiences would be described; possibly as 'the Logos conjoined with the assumed man' or even 'the assumed man conjoined with God the Logos', but the rather tentative attempts to explain this concept of 'an additive subject', as it has been called, are unconvincing. At least from the opposite standpoint they failed to provide a satisfactory bond of union and therefore there was no single subject to whom the incarnate experiences could be ascribed. Their diagnosis of duality was stronger than their provision of an adequate unity.

Modern christologies from the side of man are more radically expressed. Jesus is a man without reserve or ambiguity. The recorded human experiences must be given their full weight and nothing human, whether recorded or not, can be in principle excluded. Even if Jesus is God's Man and God's Son, nothing must detract from the recognition that he was first and foremost a man. This is of the essence and not merely of the relevance of the Incarnation. The transition from God's Son in this sense to God the Son was, according to these christologians, a false step. Even if the classical statement came to accept somewhat belatedly that every ingredient of a human nature, as it was then known, was present in the incarnate Lord, this counts for little if a genuine human individuality was absent.

This amounts to a Christology in which the primary subject

of the incarnate experiences is simply Jesus as a man. Indeed
this overriding requirement resembles a theological restrictive
practice in this type of Christology. Thus the supranaturalist
frame must be abandoned and with it the language of divine
descent and divine inbreaking. The divine self-disclosure took
place through a man utterly transparent to God in the depths
of his being; a kind of mirror image of God without refraction
or distortion. However Redemption is regarded, the theme of
divine rescue would not come readily to mind. The divine
initiative from which, on Robinson's own admission, nothing
must detract, is sufficiently safeguarded if Jesus was not an
ordinary man but the man of God's own choosing. The divine
involvement arises not from a firm Logos centre in his Person
but from his openness to the Logos or self-expressive activity
of God. Through him, still as a man, the divine activity was at
work; the divine love manifested itself. Jesus is the
Representative Man in the fullest possible sense. 'The man who
lived God' is therefore 'God for us'. His union with God is a
matter of relation, function or activity; a matter of degree, not
of kind, even if this difference of degree is strongly marked and
capable of being attractively presented.

The opposite tradition will question whether on these
premises the full implications of the Incarnation can be
effectively realised. The divine descent, the ultimate divine
condescension, the coming in person of God the Son into our
human existence for us men and for our salvation is excluded,
and this is vital alike for Revelation and Redemption. If at
times the human solidarity was played down by the classical
tradition in the supposed best interests of the divine,
christologies of this type are even more clearly exposed to the
opposite danger. The divine initiative is weakly expressed. The
divine involvement, while not negligible on this view, does not
find its maximum expression in a divine Person who unites in
himself the divine and human natures. The liquidation of the
ontological framework for Christology is a defect similar to
the omission of the supranaturalist context and perhaps even a
corollary of it. Relations and functions obviously matter in the
Incarnation but they need a better logical grounding than this
christology has so far supplied. The classical statement can

claim with good reason that they can be provided as adequately, if not better, on the ontological framework. The intention of this type of Christology is to simplify the doctrine by getting rid of the excrescences and over-elaborations of the classical statement, while claiming to retain all the essentials of Christology in a new and more contemporary idiom. Its results resemble nothing so much as a heroic but unsuccessful attempt to cut the Gordian knot.

Of the two main types of Christology studied here it will be clear that I opt without apology or reserve for a Christology from the side of God. I have always found it a good deal more difficult to decide between a full doctrine of the *Enhypostasia* of the type exemplified by Barth and the more conservative type of Kenoticism represented by Forsyth and (above all) by Weston. On balance the notion of the Logos acting at two levels of potency as the personal centre of his two disparate natures, while certainly not impossible within the framework of the theory, is faced with greater difficulties than a moderate Kenoticism which is less exposed to objection than its critics suppose. But in whichever form a Christology from the side of God is presented, its insight into the implications of the Incarnation is truer and deeper than its rival's. It retains the full paradox of the Word made flesh without attempting to reduce or to smooth it out in any way. Its statement of the central problem in Christology, the union of divine and human in a single Person, himself divinely centred, is valid on its own premises and within its own framework of thought. Since the fact is unique, it is not surprising that clarification is difficult, and adequate analogies are not forthcoming. No solution which takes full account of the character of event itself and its implications can be other than tentative.

It would be tempting to try to offer some reconciliation between the two main types of Christology. To some extent this was achieved in the Chalcedonian Definition and the classical tradition in its later developments would claim to have included what was of greatest value in the Dualist position. There are however insuperable difficulties in applying a similar 'Conciliation Procedure' to the modern developments from their classical counterparts. There are of course some overlaps arising from the subject-matter of the doctrine itself. Among these themes can be included the two solidarities with God and man, the divine initiative and involvement and to some extent the divine condescension. But these are assigned different priorities in the two christologies and the conditions of proof of true Godhead and true manhood are not identical. What satisfies one tradition seems inadequate to the other. The true humanity of the classical statement is incomplete for christologies from the side of man. The extra dimension of the classical view is readily dispensable for the rival tradition. There is no mathematical mean between addition and subtraction! The personal centring of the incarnate Lord in God the Logos or in Jesus as a man are mutually exclusive. It seems as if the divide is insuperable.

Can we then speak of a final Christology, whether from the side of God or the side of man? The short answer is a decided negative. This is not merely because no intellectual framework is endowed with the divine attribute of immutability, but arises from the inexhaustible character of the Incarnation itself. Adherents of a Christology from the side of God would claim that the uniqueness of the Incarnation must ultimately transcend human efforts to grasp it completely. What God has done is greater than man can comprehend by the intellect alone. As an arithmetician might put it, Godhead into manhood won't go, and yet has gone! A 'final Christology' will for ever elude us. To succeed in Christology is only not to fail too badly. It is not that we have failed to think hard enough or are not clever enough, though God knows that both may well be true, but that the fact itself is too big for human comprehension and does not admit of a neat and tidy solution which answers all the questions and solves all the problems. The opposing charges of over-provision and understatement remind us of the difficulty and delicacy of our quest.

That is why words like mystery and paradox, however unfashionable they may be in the present thought-climate, are important for Christology. It was the merit of Baron von Hügel, the lay Roman Catholic philosopher and theologian, to distinguish between the 'rich', that which might appear obscure through the excess of its subject-matter over the intellectual constructions which attempt to explore it, and the 'clear', in which the tools of thought are entirely adequate for their purpose. Another Roman Catholic philosopher, Gabriel Marcel, drew a similar distinction between genuine mysteries which liberate the spirit and mere puzzles which tease and hurt the mind. The doctrine of the Incarnation belongs to the first pair of terms and not the second.

In quite different circles the idea of paradox has been regarded as a kind of signature of divine action. There is, for example, a paradox of Creation and of Grace as well as a paradox of the Incarnation. Christologies from the side of man suspect here a surreptitious and illicit attempt to restore the 'missing dimension'. At least in much recent thinking about the Incarnation these notes are singularly lacking. Professor R. W. Hepburn, a leading humanist, in his book *Christianity and Paradox*, and Professor Steven Katz in his essay 'The language and logic of "mystery" in Christology' (*Christ, Faith and History*; ed. S. W. Sykes and J. P. Clayton, Cambridge University Press, 1972, pp. 239–63) criticise these approaches on their own premises.

Nevertheless the use of this type of language seems fruitful for Christology. It is not a direct appeal to the irrational, otherwise Christology could not have got started at all, but a realistic assessment that there are limits beyond which human thought cannot carry us, while its subject-matter goes on. It is not the 'murder of logic' but an admission that human logic is not omnicompetent in the expression of divine truth. The much-vaunted 'intellectual rigour', in the interests of which such appeals are deplored, may mask a spiritual unperceptiveness which its conditions of proof and intellectual framework necessitates. It is a wise maxim of theology that 'all things issue in mysteries', but that does not justify us in taking mystery as our starting-point. We must examine and assess the evidence, test rival possibilities for adequacy, take our understanding of the issues involved as far as it will go and then know why we can go as far as this and no further. We can show good reason for preferring one doctrinal formulation to another and for regarding it as a closer approximation to the reality which we are trying to explore. We can, as it were, arbitrate between penultimate christologies without claiming that the last word has been or can be said.

Here too the classical statement has a clear lead over its rivals not only in what it tries to include in its christology but also in explaining why a final solution cannot be expected. It is my profound belief that christologies from the side of God give a more God-worthy content to the Incarnation than their rivals. They explain better why it still has the character of a genuine mystery and not a mere logical puzzle. They match more readily what we can glimpse of the divine intention both in Revelation and Redemption. They give stronger support than their rivals to the double acclamation of Christ as 'My Lord and my God' and yet 'My Saviour and my brother' which is the goal of every believing Christian and the witness of the Church in worship, faith and practice.

Index

133